Decadent Desserts

Experience one of life's sweetest pleasures—dessert! Tupperware is excited to introduce you to our special collection of delectable desserts. In this book, you'll find delicious recipes to fit every occasion, from finishing touches for family fare to party-perfect productions. In a hurry? Take advantage of our time-minded temptations. Counting calories? Then indulge in our slimmed-down sweets. Whatever your pleasure, our easy embellishing ideas will ensure that all your desserts look as enticing as the Chocolate Shortbread-Raspberry Torte shown on the cover.

This seal assures you that every recipe in **Decadent Desserts** has been tested in the *Better Homes and Gardens*® Test Kitchen. This means that each recipe is practical and reliable, and meets high standards of taste appeal.

All microwave tests were completed in a variety of high-wattage microwave ovens. Cooking times are approximate since microwave ovens vary by manufacturer.

Tupperware™

Contents

Easy
Embellishments

Embellishing your desserts will make sure your homemade creations never look homely. Even the simplest of garnishes will transform a plain-looking dessert into an enchanting finish to a meal. On the next few pages, you'll find everything you need for picture-perfect presentations. Check out our techniques, then put your creativity to work!

Getting started

Beautiful desserts begin with a few basics. Try these suggestions to help turn ordinary desserts into works of art.

- Keep it simple. Use a single garnish for maximum effect.
- Play it again. Select a garnish that repeats or complements a flavor or ingredient in the dessert.
- Add to the allure. Pick your prettiest or most spectacular dishes for the presentation. A pedestal cake plate, for example, elevates a humble cake to the ranks of the exalted.
- Keep on trying. If your first attempts are less than spectacular, don't give up. Practice improves results.

Successful strategies

Often, the easiest garnishes are the most striking. Here are ideas for fast flourishes:

Fruits are a natural for garnishing desserts. Choose from whole strawberries or raspberries, grapes, kiwi slices, and orange, lemon, and lime slices or strips of peel. Get fancy—cut strawberries into fans or create a flower using a cluster of raspberries and fresh mint leaves.

Toasted coconut or nuts add a tasty accent to almost any dessert. Arrange pecan halves, walnut halves, whole hazelnuts, or whole almonds on desserts. Or, sprinkle with chopped nuts or coconut. (To toast nuts or coconut, spread in a thin layer on a baking sheet or in a shallow baking pan. Bake in a 350° oven for 5 to 10 minutes or until golden brown, stirring once or twice and checking often.)

Edible flowers make easy, elegant garnishes. Scatter small flowers or sprinkle some petals over a dessert. Especially good with sweets are pansies, violets, rose petals, dianthus, and daylilies. For freshest flavor, pick edible flowers just before using, rinse, and gently pat dry. Keep in mind that for a flower to be edible, it must be free of all toxins—both natural and synthetic. Remember, also, that not all flowers are edible and that not all parts of edible flowers are safe to eat.

Powdered sugar or unsweetened cocoa powder can be sprinkled over desserts for a fast finish. Just spoon the powdered sugar or cocoa into a sieve or sifter. Then lightly tap the utensil as you move it over the entire surface of the dessert. For a heavier coating, dust again. To add more drama, use powdered sugar or cocoa for stenciling. Use a purchased doily or stencil or make your own stencil from lightweight cardboard. Place the stencil on top of the dessert and sift powdered sugar or cocoa over the stencil. When finished dusting the dessert, carefully lift off the stencil.

Tools of the Trade

Guarantee great results when you use Tupperware® brand products to make and store your desserts.

Measuring liquids has never been easier than with the Tupperware 2-cup Measuring pitcher. For accurately measuring dry ingredients, use the Measuring Cup Set. For small amounts of liquid or dry ingredients, use the Measuring Spoon Set.

Tupperware bowls are perfect for mixing. The New Mixing Bowl comes with a splatter guard, and its nonskid base is specially designed to stay put on your counter.

Pastry projects are a cinch with the Tupperware® Pastry sheet and Rolling Pin. A screw-off cap lets you fill the Rolling Pin with cold water.

Rely on the Tupperware® vegetable peeler to create chocolate shavings and curls. Or, use the Vegetable Peeler to cut strips of orange, lemon, or lime peel for garnishing.

For storing your completed dessert masterpieces, turn to the Tupperware® Maxi-Cake taker, 10" Cake Taker, Fresh-N-Fancy® container, and 12" Pie Taker.

Pastry Pointers

You don't have to hire a professional pastry chef to create pretty-as-a-picture pastries. Here are a few time-tested ideas for preparing pastries that look every bit as good as they taste. (See pages 42 and 45 for recipes for one-crust and two-crust pastries.)

Scalloped edge: Trim and turn under the edge of the pastry for a single- or double-crust pie. Make a large scallop by placing your thumb flat against the inside pastry edge and pressing the dough around the thumb of one hand with the thumb and index finger of your other hand.

Dotted pastry top: Prepare a double-crust pie, *except* do not cut slits in the top crust. Instead, use a wooden skewer or toothpick to prick a design in the pastry, enlarging each hole so steam can escape. Press the edge with the tines of a fork to seal.

Cutout edge: Trim pastry to the edge of the pie plate for a single-crust pie. Roll out pastry scraps very thin. Use a knife or a miniature cookie or canapé cutter to cut the pastry into desired shapes. Brush the edge of the pastry shell with water. Arrange the cutouts on the edge of the pastry shell and lightly press to secure.

Quick lattice top: Prepare a double-crust pie, *except* do not cut slits in the top crust. Use a miniature cookie or canapé cutter to make a cutout in center of the dough. Repeat cuts in a regular pattern, working from the center to the edge. Be careful not to make the cutouts too close together, or the pastry may rip when transferred to the pie. Wrap the the pastry around a rolling pin to transfer to the pie. Trim and crimp the edge.

Flower-petal edge: Make a scalloped edge, fluting as directed above. Press fork tines lightly in the center of each scallop.

Herringbone lattice top: Prepare a double-crust pie, *except* do not cut slits in the top crust. Use a fluted pastry wheel to cut pastry into ½-inch-wide strips. Arrange two strips crosswise in center of pie. Then arrange pastry strips to form a small square in the center of the pie. Begin a second, larger square ½ inch from the first square.

Continue placing pastry strips to form progressively larger squares. Trim pastry. Fold strips under bottom pastry to make a smooth raised edge. Flute.

Rickrack edge: Make a scalloped edge, fluting as directed above. Using your fingers and a thumb, pinch the edge of each scallop as shown to form a narrow point.

Piping Techniques

Personalize your cakes, tortes, and other desserts by piping frosting, whipped cream, or melted chocolate in a variety of designs. All you need is a decorating bag and a few decorating tips. Then turn your imagination loose and watch your personal creations come alive.

Decorating bags: Purchased cloth, plastic-lined, or disposable plastic decorator bags are available in different sizes and materials. Or make your own decorating bag from a heavy clear plastic bag simply by snipping off one of the bottom corners to make a small hole in the bag. For dots, lines, and writing, just squeeze the frosting through the hole. For shells, leaves, and other intricate designs, fit the appropriate decorating tip into the plastic bag.

Holding the bag:

Proper technique is essential for successful piping. After you've fit the desired tip into the decorating bag, fill the bag about half full of frosting. Then fold the corners over and roll the bag down to the frosting. With your writing hand, grip the bag near the roll above the frosting level. Then apply pressure from the palm of your hand, forcing frosting toward the tip. Use your other hand to guide the tip of the bag.

Decorating-bag tips: These come in many shapes and sizes, but with just three tips—a round tip, a star tip, and a leaf tip—you can make beautifully decorated desserts. Use small- or medium-size tips for piping frosting or melted chocolate; use larger tips for whipped cream.

- **Round tips** have simple round openings and are used for writing and to create dots and lines.

For writing and making dots and lines, hold the bag at a 45-degree angle just above the surface of the dessert. To end each letter or line, gently touch the tip to the surface, stop pressure, and pull away.

For dots, hold the bag at a 90-degree angle with the tip almost touching the dessert surface. Squeeze out a dot of frosting until it's the size you want, then stop applying pressure and pull away.

- **Star tips** are used to make shells and zigzags, as well as stars.

For stars, hold the bag at a 90-degree angle with the tip just above the dessert surface. Squeeze out some frosting, stop applying pressure, then pull away.

For shells, hold the bag at a 45-degree angle just above the surface of the dessert. Squeeze out some frosting until you've formed a mound. Push the tip down and away from the mound until it touches the surface and forms a tail. Stop applying pressure and pull away. Start the next shell at the stopping point of the previous one (shells will overlap slightly).

For zigzags, hold the bag at a 45-degree angle to the dessert surface. Touch the top to the surface; squeeze out frosting as you move the tip from side to side. Stop pressure and pull away.

- **Leaf tips** are great for making leaves. Hold the bag at a 45-degree angle, keeping the top opening parallel to the dessert surface. Squeeze out some frosting to make the base of a leaf. Continue squeezing, but ease up on the pressure as you pull away. Stop pressure and lift off, forming a tip.

Chocolate Creations

Chocolate—it's the ultimate dessert and the ultimate dessert garnish. Chocolate embellishments can be as simple as a sprinkling of shaved chocolate or as sophisticated as a crown of chocolate curls. Find out everything you need to know about garnishing with chocolate on these two pages.

Grated chocolate: Use semisweet, sweet, or milk chocolate, or a white baking bar. To grate, rub a solid piece of chocolate across the fine or large grating section of a hand-held grater.

Shaved chocolate: Start with semisweet chocolate, sweet chocolate, milk chocolate, or a white baking bar. Using a vegetable peeler such as the Tupperware® vegetable peeler, make short, quick strokes across the surface of a solid piece of chocolate.

Small chocolate curls: Easiest to make with milk chocolate, small chocolate curls also can be made with a white baking bar. Let chocolate come to room temperature, then draw a vegetable peeler across the bar. For small curls, use the narrow side of the chocolate piece, and for large curls, use the wide surface.

Tempered chocolate: If you work with tempered chocolate, you can create an even wider variety of chocolate garnishes. This method of melting and cooling chocolate stabilizes it so the garnishes you create will hold their shape at room temperature.

When you don't have time to temper chocolate, substitute chocolate-flavored candy coating or a white baking bar. Just chop and, using very low heat, melt on the rangetop or in the microwave oven. Don't add vegetable shortening.

Follow these steps to temper semisweet chocolate, then try your hand at dipping chocolate and at making chocolate leaves, chocolate cutouts, chocolate lace, and large chocolate curls.

- Chop up to 1 pound of chocolate into small pieces. Or use packaged chocolate pieces. In a 4-cup glass measure or 1½-quart glass mixing bowl combine chocolate and shortening. (Use 1 tablespoon vegetable shortening for every 6 ounces chocolate.) In a large glass mixing bowl, pour very warm tap water (100° to 110°) to a depth of 1 inch. Place the glass measure or bowl containing chocolate inside the larger bowl. Water should cover the bottom half of measure or bowl containing chocolate.

- Stir the chocolate mixture *constantly* with a rubber spatula until the chocolate mixture is completely melted and smooth. This takes about 15 to 20 minutes; don't rush the process. If the water begins to cool, remove measure or bowl containing chocolate. Discard the cool water; add warm water. Return the measure or bowl containing chocolate to the bowl containing the water.

- Avoid getting *any* water in chocolate. Just one drop can cause chocolate to become dull and grainy. If water gets into chocolate, stir in additional *vegetable shortening*, 1 teaspoon at a time, until mixture becomes shiny and smooth.

- When melted and smooth, the chocolate is ready for shaping or dipping. If the chocolate becomes too thick during handling, replace the water in larger bowl, as directed above. Stir chocolate constantly until it again reaches desired consistency.

Let your finished product set up in a cool, dry place. *Do not chill* your finished product, or the chocolate will lose temper and become soft at room temperature.

Chocolate leaves: You'll need chemical-free nontoxic fresh leaves—try mint, lemon, ivy, rose, or strawberry leaves—and a clean, small paintbrush. For 12 small leaves, use 2 ounces tempered chocolate or melted white baking bar or candy coating.

Using the paintbrush, brush one or two coats of chocolate on the underside of each leaf. Wipe away any chocolate from the top side of the leaf. Then place the leaves, chocolate side up, on a baking sheet lined with waxed paper or a curved surface (such as the Tupperware rolling pin or the bottom edge of a pie plate) until dry. Before using, peel the leaf away from the chocolate.

Chocolate cutouts: Pour tempered chocolate or melted white baking bar or candy coating onto a baking sheet lined with waxed paper and spread it ⅛ to ¼ inch thick. Let stand until almost dry. Firmly press miniature cookie or canapé cutters into the chocolate. Then carefully lift the cutouts from the waxed paper.

Chocolate lace: Using tempered chocolate or melted white baking bar or candy coating (or a combination of them), pipe or drizzle small designs on a baking sheet lined with waxed paper. Let the garnishes stand until dry or chill them in the freezer for five minutes, then remove by carefully peeling them from the waxed paper.

Large chocolate curls: Temper 2 ounces of chocolate with 1 teaspoon of shortening as directed on the opposite page. (Or melt 2 ounces white baking bar or candy coating.) Set aside.

Heat a 3-quart rectangular baking dish in a 350° oven for 2 minutes. Remove dish from oven and place upside down on a thick towel to protect work surface. Cool the dish until it is about the same temperature as the chocolate.

Using a narrow metal spatula, spread chocolate over the entire surface of the inverted dish. Let stand until the chocolate is firm, but not hard. Hold the blade of a metal pancake turner at a 30-degree angle; push the blade away from you, scraping the chocolate off the dish. Use the turner to lift the curls from the dish, being careful not to touch the curls with your fingers because the curls can soften easily.

Chocolate-dipped decorations: You can dip a variety of garnishes, including strawberries, nuts, and cookies into chocolate for an extra-special effect. Dip desired garnish into tempered chocolate or melted white baking bar or candy coating. Dip the entire garnish or half the garnish. For small nuts, such as hazelnuts, use a clean, small paintbrush to brush on the chocolate. Let the garnishes stand on waxed paper until the chocolate is dry.

Storing garnishes: Keep extra chocolate garnishes fresh in airtight freezer containers such as the Tupperware® Freezer Mates® containers. That way you can add flair to desserts on a moment's notice. Simply cut a piece of waxed paper and place in the bottom of a container. Then arrange chocolate leaves, cutouts, curls, or lace in a single layer on top of the waxed paper. Seal and freeze for up to three months. To remove, carefully peel the garnishes off the waxed paper. Chocolate-dipped nuts and cookies also store nicely in freezer containers in single layers.

Chocolate
Show-Stoppers

Indulge—in the decadence of a luscious chocolate dessert. In this chapter, you'll find everything you need to satisfy your craving for chocolate, from irresistible Walnut Fudge Pudding Cake to elegant White Chocolate-Coconut Cake. Can you think of a happier ending for any meal?

White Chocolate-Coconut Cake
(See recipe, page 12.)

White Chocolate-Coconut Cake

Per serving:
622 cal. (39% from fat), 8 g pro., 89 g carbo., 27 g fat,
91 mg cholesterol, 1 g dietary fiber, 286 mg sodium.

Preparation time:
25 minutes

Baking time:
30 minutes

Cooling time:
1½ hours

Garnish this classy cake with chocolate leaves, as shown on pages 10–11. Make the white and dark chocolate leaves using the directions on page 9.

5 egg whites

2 cups all-purpose flour

1 tablespoon baking powder

¼ teaspoon salt

4 ounces white baking bar, chopped

1 cup milk

½ cup margarine or butter

1¼ cups sugar

1½ teaspoons vanilla

5 egg yolks

½ cup coconut

½ cup finely chopped pecans

Creamy White Frosting (see tip, below)

¼ cup coconut

Chocolate Leaves (see directions, page 9) (optional)

- Place egg whites in a large mixing bowl; let stand at room temperature for 30 minutes. Grease and lightly flour two 9x1½-inch round baking pans; set aside. Stir together flour, baking powder, and salt; set aside.

- Combine white baking bar and ⅓ cup of the milk in a small heavy saucepan; heat over very low heat, stirring constantly, until baking bar begins to melt. Immediately remove from heat and stir until smooth. Stir in the remaining milk and set aside to cool.

- Beat margarine with electric mixer on medium speed 30 seconds or until softened. Add sugar and vanilla; beat to combine. Add yolks, one at a time, beating after each. Alternately add flour mixture and baking bar mixture, beating on low speed after each addition to combine.

- Thoroughly wash beaters. Beat egg whites until stiff peaks form (tips stand straight). Gently fold whites into batter. Gently fold in the ½ cup coconut and the pecans. Spread batter in prepared pans. Bake in a 350° oven for 30 to 35 minutes or until wooden toothpick inserted near center comes out clean. Cool cakes in pans on wire rack for 10 minutes. Remove from pans; cool completely.

- Place ¾ cup of the Creamy White Frosting in a small bowl; stir in the ¼ cup coconut. To assemble cake, place one cake layer on a large serving plate. Spread with the frosting-coconut mixture. Top with the remaining cake layer. Frost with remaining plain frosting. Garnish with Chocolate Leaves, if desired. Makes 12 servings.

Note: Pictured on pages 10–11.

Creamy White Frosting

Whip up this rich, decadent frosting and instantly add pizzazz to any two-layer chocolate cake.

Chop 4 ounces *white baking bar*. Combine chopped baking bar and ¼ cup *milk* in a small heavy saucepan; heat over very low heat, stirring constantly, until the baking bar begins to melt. Immediately remove from heat; stir until smooth. Cool. Sift 1 pound *powdered sugar* (4¾ cups sifted). Beat ⅓ cup *margarine* or *butter* in a mixing bowl until fluffy. Gradually beat in the melted baking bar, *2 cups* of the powdered sugar, and 1½ teaspoons *vanilla*. Slowly beat in the remaining powdered sugar and, if necessary, additional milk (1 to 2 tablespoons) to make of spreading consistency.

Apricot-Glazed Chocolate Nut Cake

Per serving:
385 cal. (42% from fat), 8 g pro., 49 g carbo., 19 g fat,
133 mg cholesterol, 3 g dietary fiber, 112 mg sodium.

Preparation time:
15 minutes

Baking time:
35 minutes

Cooling time:
1½ hours

Chilling time:
2 hours

For an easy, yet elegant dessert, whip up this flourless chocolate cake in your blender or food processor. Embellish with apricots and a sweet-tart apricot glaze.

1½ cups broken walnuts or pecans

¾ cup sugar

¼ cup unsweetened cocoa powder

¼ cup semisweet chocolate pieces

1 teaspoon baking powder

¼ teaspoon baking soda

5 eggs

1 teaspoon vanilla

3 apricots, pitted and sliced, or one 8-ounce can unpeeled apricot halves, drained and sliced

Apricot Glaze (see recipe at right)

• Grease and flour a 9-inch springform pan. Combine broken nuts, sugar, cocoa powder, chocolate pieces, baking powder, and baking soda in a blender container or food processor bowl. Cover and blend or process until nuts are ground. Add eggs and vanilla. Blend or process until *nearly* smooth.

• Spread nut mixture in the prepared pan. Bake in a 350° oven for 35 minutes or until the cake tests done. Cool in springform pan on a wire rack for 10 minutes. Remove sides of springform pan. Cool completely. Place the cake on a serving platter. Arrange apricot slices on top of the cake. Top with Apricot Glaze. Chill for 2 hours before serving. Makes 8 to 10 servings.

Apricot Glaze: Combine ⅔ cup *apricot preserves* and 2 teaspoons *cornstarch* in a small saucepan. (Cut up any large pieces of fruit.) Stir in 2 tablespoons *brandy* or *orange juice*. Cook, stirring constantly, until bubbly. Cook and stir for 2 minutes more. Cover surface with waxed paper. Cool without stirring.

Caramel-Chocolate Pecan Pie

Per serving:
634 cal. (59% from fat), 10 g pro., 59 g carbo., 43 g fat,
124 mg cholesterol, 3 g dietary fiber, 243 mg sodium.

Preparation time:
15 minutes

Baking time:
45 minutes

Chilling time:
1 hour

Hidden under a layer of cheesecake is a delicious surprise—a mixture of chocolate, caramel, and pecans.

1 cup pecan pieces

Pastry for a 9-inch one-crust pie (see tips, pages 44 and 45)

1 6-ounce package semisweet chocolate pieces (1 cup)

½ cup caramel ice-cream topping

1 8-ounce package cream cheese, softened

1 8-ounce carton dairy sour cream

½ cup sugar

1 teaspoon vanilla

3 eggs

Unsweetened cocoa powder (optional)

• Sprinkle pecan pieces evenly in unbaked piecrust; sprinkle with chocolate pieces and drizzle with caramel topping. Set aside.

• Beat cream cheese, sour cream, sugar, and vanilla in a medium mixing bowl until smooth. Add eggs, beating on low speed of an electric mixer just until combined. Pour over caramel topping in piecrust. Bake in a 350° oven about 45 minutes or until center appears set. Cool on a wire rack. Chill, covered, for at least 1 hour before serving. Sift cocoa powder lightly over pie, if desired. Makes 8 to 10 servings.

French Silk Pie

Per serving:
535 cal. (64% from fat), 6 g pro., 44 g carbo., 40 g fat,
147 mg cholesterol, 2 g dietary fiber, 274 mg sodium.

Preparation time:
25 minutes

Baking time:
10 minutes

Chilling time:
5 hours

Whipped cream and grated chocolate crown this classic chocolate pie. It's so rich, you'll need to cut it into slivers to serve.

Pastry for a 9-inch one-crust pie (see tips, pages 44 and 45)

1 cup sugar

¾ cup butter (do not use margarine)

3 ounces unsweetened chocolate, melted and cooled

1 teaspoon vanilla

¾ cup refrigerated or frozen egg substitute, thawed

½ cup whipping cream

Grated unsweetened chocolate

- Prick bottom and sides of piecrust generously with tines of fork, including where bottom and sides meet. Bake in a 450° oven for 10 to 12 minutes or until golden. Cool on a wire rack.

- Beat the sugar and butter with an electric mixer on medium speed about 4 minutes or until fluffy. Stir in the melted chocolate and the vanilla. Add egg substitute *¼ cup* at a time, beating on high speed after each addition and scraping sides of bowl constantly. Spoon filling into the baked piecrust. Cover and chill in the refrigerator for 5 to 24 hours before serving.

- To serve, whip cream *just until* stiff peaks form. Spoon whipped cream into a decorating bag fitted with a large star tip (about ½-inch opening). Pipe on top of chocolate filling in a decorative pattern. (Or spoon whipped cream over the chocolate filling.) Sprinkle grated chocolate over whipped cream. Use a hot knife to cut the pie. Makes 10 servings.

Egg Enlightenment

Traditionally, French Silk Pie called for a filling made with uncooked eggs. Our recipe uses egg substitute instead. Why? Because eating raw or only slightly cooked eggs is a potential food hazard—bacterial contamination from salmonella could occur, resulting in food poisoning. Those particularly susceptible include the elderly, infants, pregnant women, and people already ill, although anyone can get sick. So we opted to come up with a recipe that offers none of the risk, but all of the pleasure.

Even when cooking eggs use precautions. Always cook eggs to the firm stage—they should reach a final temperature of 160° or remain at 140° for at least 3½ minutes. When separating eggs, never use the shell-to-shell method; instead, use an egg separator—or your hands. How? Starting with clean hands, pour the whole egg into your palm, then let the white slip through your fingers while keeping the yolk in your hand. It's easy (many cooks even think fun) and safe.

French Silk Pie

Black Walnut-Chocolate Pie

Per serving:
551 cal. (47% from fat), 9 g pro., 68 g carbo., 30 g fat, 80 mg cholesterol, 2 g dietary fiber, 205 mg sodium.

Preparation time:
12 minutes

Baking time:
40 minutes

Chilling time:
1 hour

Black walnuts lend distinctive flavor to this chocolaty pie. Black walnuts aren't as commonly available as English walnuts, but usually can be found in larger supermarkets.

3 eggs

1 cup light corn syrup

½ cup sugar

⅓ cup margarine or butter, melted

1 cup black walnut or hickory nut pieces

½ cup miniature semisweet chocolate pieces

Pastry for a 9-inch one-crust pie (see tips, page 44 and 45)

Whipped cream (optional)

- For filling, lightly beat eggs in a medium mixing bowl just until combined. Stir in corn syrup, sugar, and melted margarine. Mix well. Stir in black walnuts. Set filling aside.

- Sprinkle chocolate pieces over bottom of piecrust. With pie plate on oven rack, pour filling into crust.

- To prevent overbrowning, cover edge of pie with foil. Bake in a 350° oven for 20 minutes. Remove foil. Bake 20 to 25 minutes more or until a knife inserted near center of pie comes out clean. Cool on a wire rack. Chill, covered, for at least 1 hour before serving. Spoon whipped cream on top before serving, if desired. Makes 8 to 10 servings.

Candy Bar Pie

Per serving:
451 cal. (69% from fat), 6 g pro., 31 g carbo., 36 g fat, 46 mg cholesterol, 2 g dietary fiber, 79 mg sodium.

Preparation time:
25 minutes

Baking time:
10 minutes

Cooling time:
30 minutes

Freezing time:
5 hours

You'd never dream that this exquisite milk-chocolate pie was made with melted marshmallows! Make it up to two months ahead and store in the Tupperware® 12" pie taker in the freezer.

6 1- to 1½-ounce bars milk chocolate with almonds, chopped

15 large marshmallows or 1½ cups tiny marshmallows

½ cup milk

1 cup whipping cream

½ teaspoon vanilla

Walnut Crust (see recipe, below right)

Whipped cream (optional)

Coarsely chopped milk chocolate bars with almonds (optional)

- Combine the 6 candy bars, the marshmallows, and milk in a medium saucepan; heat and stir over medium-low heat until chocolate is melted. Remove from heat; cool to room temperature.

- Meanwhile, chill a large mixing bowl and beaters. In the chilled bowl beat whipping cream and vanilla with an electric mixer on medium speed until soft peaks form (tips curl). Fold into cooled chocolate mixture. Spoon chocolate mixture into Walnut Crust. Freeze pie about 5 hours or until firm.

- To serve, let pie stand at room temperature for 10 minutes before cutting into wedges. Top each serving with whipped cream and additional chopped candy bars, if desired. Makes 8 to 10 servings.

Walnut Crust: Combine 1½ cups coarsely ground *walnut*s (6 ounces), 3 tablespoons melted *margarine* or *butter*, and 2 tablespoons *sugar* in a medium mixing bowl. Press nut mixture firmly onto bottom and up sides of a 9-inch pie plate. Bake in a 325° oven about 10 minutes or until edge is golden. Cool on a wire rack.

Choco-Peanut Butter Pie

Per serving:
451 cal. (36% from fat), 7 g pro., 68 g carbo., 19 g fat,
80 mg cholesterol, 2 g dietary fiber, 193 mg sodium.

Preparation time:
10 minutes

Baking time:
35 minutes

Chilling time:
1 hour

Kids—of all ages—will love this scrumptious pie. Think of it as a peanut butter and chocolate version of pecan pie.

3 eggs

1 cup light corn syrup

½ cup sugar

⅓ cup chunky-style peanut butter

½ teaspoon vanilla

½ cup semisweet chocolate pieces

Pastry for a 9-inch one-crust pie (see tips, pages 44 and 45)

Whipped dessert topping (optional)

Semisweet chocolate pieces (optional)

Chopped peanuts (optional)

- For filling, beat eggs lightly with a rotary beater or a fork until combined. Stir in corn syrup, sugar, peanut butter, and vanilla. Mix well.

- Sprinkle the ½ cup chocolate pieces over the bottom of piecrust. Pour filling into crust.

- To prevent overbrowning, cover edge of pie with foil. Bake in a 375° oven for 20 minutes. Remove foil. Bake for 15 to 20 minutes more or until a knife inserted near the center comes out clean. Cool on wire rack. Chill, covered, for at least 1 hour before serving. Garnish with whipped topping, additional chocolate pieces, and peanuts, if desired. Makes 8 to 10 servings.

Chocolate Choices

What do all the recipes in this chapter have in common? Chocolate. But not every recipe uses the same kind of chocolate. Here's what's what:

Unsweetened cocoa powder—pure chocolate with most of the cocoa butter removed.
Unsweetened chocolate—pure chocolate with no sugar or flavorings added. Also called bitter or baking chocolate.
Semisweet chocolate—made of chocolate, extra cocoa butter, and sugar.
Sweet baking chocolate—sweeter than semisweet. Made of pure chocolate, extra cocoa butter, and sugar.
Milk chocolate—made of pure chocolate with extra cocoa butter, sugar, and milk solids.
White baking bar—not a true chocolate because it lacks chocolate solids. Sold in boxes next to baking chocolate.
Candy coating—has most cocoa butter replaced by other fat. Flavored with vanilla or other flavorings.

Chocolate Truffle Cups

Chocolate Truffle Cups

Per serving:
452 cal. (68% from fat), 5 g pro., 32 g carbo., 35 g fat,
55 mg cholesterol, 2 g dietary fiber, 88 mg sodium.

Preparation time:
30 minutes

Chilling times:
1 hour; 1½ hours;
2 hours

Standing time:
15 minutes

Impress dinner guests with this luscious dessert. For preparation, it's best to make the candy cups and the garnish a few days ahead. Then, the day before your dinner, prepare the filling and pipe it into the cups. Add the garnish at serving time.

5 ounces white baking bar, chopped

3 tablespoons ground toasted almonds

6 ounces semisweet chocolate, cut up

½ cup whipping cream

¼ cup margarine or butter

1 beaten egg yolk

3 tablespoons whipping cream

Chocolate Lace (see directions, page 9)

- For candy cups, arrange 6 foil bake cups inside muffin tins for support. Melt the white baking bar in a small heavy saucepan over very low heat, stirring constantly until baking bar starts to melt. Immediately remove from heat and stir until baking bar is completely melted and smooth. Stir in the ground almonds. Spoon *1 rounded tablespoon* of the mixture into *each* of the foil bake cups. With pastry brush or small spatula, spread mixture over bottoms and up sides of cups. Chill until hardened (about 1 hour). Remove foil from candy cups. To store, place in a single layer in a Tupperware® container or another container; cover and chill for up to 3 days.

- For filling, combine semisweet chocolate, the ½ cup whipping cream, and the margarine in a heavy saucepan. Cook and stir over low heat until chocolate is melted. Gradually stir *about half* of the hot mixture into the egg yolk. Return all of the mixture to the saucepan. Cook and stir just until mixture starts to bubble. Remove from heat. Stir in the 3 tablespoons whipping cream. Transfer chocolate mixture to a small bowl. Cover and chill *just* until mixture is smooth and thickened (about 1½ hours), stirring occasionally. (The butter may separate but will blend in when the mixture is stirred.)

- Beat the chilled chocolate mixture with an electric mixer on medium speed about 2 minutes or until light and fluffy. Spoon the chocolate mixture into a decorating bag fitted with a large star tip (about ¾-inch opening). Pipe chocolate mixture into candy cups. Cover and chill for 2 to 24 hours.

- Before serving, let stand at room temperature for 15 to 20 minutes. Garnish each serving with Chocolate Lace. Makes 6 servings.

Nicely Toasted Nuts

Desserts, such as the Chocolate Truffle Cups featured above, taste even better when you toast the nuts. Spread the nuts in a thin layer on an ungreased baking sheet or shallow baking pan. Bake in a 350° oven for 5 to 10 minutes or until the nuts are golden brown, stirring once or twice and checking often to keep from burning. You can toast more nuts than you need and store the extra in freezer containers, such as the Tupperware® Freezer Mates® containers.

Raspberry Truffle Cake

Per serving:
407 cal. (54% from fat), 4 g pro., 46 g carbo., 26 g fat,
112 mg cholesterol, 3 g dietary fiber, 110 mg sodium.

Preparation time:
15 minutes

Baking time:
25 minutes

Cooling time:
2 hours

Chilling time:
4 hours

Talk about decadent! This nearly flourless cake uses a whole pound of semisweet chocolate. It may seem soft after baking, but it firms up as it chills.

16	ounces semisweet chocolate, cut up
½	cup butter (do not use margarine)
1	tablespoon sugar
1½	teaspoons all-purpose flour
1	teaspoon raspberry liqueur (optional)
4	egg yolks
4	egg whites
1	12-ounce jar seedless raspberry jam (1 cup)
	Whipped cream

- Grease an 8-inch springform pan.

- Combine chocolate and butter in a large heavy saucepan. Cook and stir over low heat until chocolate melts. Remove from heat. Stir in sugar, flour, and, if desired, liqueur. Using a spoon, beat in egg yolks, one at a time, until combined. Set aside.

- Beat egg whites with an electric mixer on high speed until stiff peaks form (tips stand straight). Fold into chocolate mixture. Pour into prepared springform pan. Bake in a 350° oven for 25 to 30 minutes or until edges puff. Cool on wire rack for 30 minutes. Remove sides of pan; cool completely. Cover and chill for 4 to 24 hours.

- Heat jam just until melted. Slice cake. For each serving, drizzle some jam on a dessert plate; top with a cake slice and a spoonful of whipped cream. Makes 12 servings.

Spiced Chocolate Tea Cakes

Per serving:
74 cal. (41% from fat), 1 g pro., 10 g carbo., 3 g fat,
7 mg cholesterol, 0 g dietary fiber, 30 mg sodium.

Preparation time:
15 minutes

Baking time:
12 minutes

Cooling time:
30 minutes

Use a decorating bag and a large star tip to shape the dough for these tiny tea cakes into shells. Delicious with freshly brewed coffee or tea!

1½	cups all-purpose flour
¼	cup unsweetened cocoa powder
¼	teaspoon baking powder
¼	teaspoon ground nutmeg or ground cardamom
½	cup margarine or butter
¾	cup granulated sugar
1	egg yolk
⅓	cup milk
	Sifted powdered sugar

- Grease 2 baking sheets.

- Stir together flour, cocoa powder, baking powder, and nutmeg or cardamom in a small mixing bowl. Set aside.

- Beat margarine with an electric mixer on medium speed for 30 seconds; add granulated sugar and beat until fluffy. Beat in egg yolk. Add about *half* of the flour mixture. Add milk and beat until well blended. Beat or stir in the remaining flour mixture. (If dough is too stiff to pipe, stir in additional milk, a teaspoon at a time, until dough is of piping consistency.)

- Spoon dough into a decorating bag fitted with a large star tip (about ½-inch opening). Pipe dough into 1½-inch shells on prepared baking sheets, pulling the decorating bag toward you as you pipe.

- Bake tea cakes in a 350° oven for 12 to 14 minutes or until set. Cool on baking sheets for 1 minute. Remove and cool on wire racks. Sift powdered sugar over tea cakes. Makes about 30 tea cakes.

Chocolate Chiffon Cake

Per serving:
446 cal. (53% from fat), 6 g pro., 46 g carbo., 27 g fat,
147 mg cholesterol, 2 g dietary fiber, 170 mg sodium.

Preparation time:
25 minutes

Baking time:
50 minutes

Cooling time:
1½ hours

Be sure to cool the chiffon loaf upside down for the lightest, fluffiest cake possible. If your cake rises above the loaf pan, cool it by inverting the cake in the pan with its edges resting on two other pans of equal height.

⅓	cup water
2	ounces unsweetened chocolate
2	tablespoons granulated sugar
1	cup sifted all-purpose flour
¾	cup granulated sugar
1½	teaspoons baking powder
⅓	cup cooking oil
4	egg yolks
⅓	cup cold water
½	teaspoon vanilla
4	egg whites
½	teaspoon cream of tartar
	Mint Topping (see recipe at right)

● Combine the first 3 ingredients in a saucepan. Heat and stir over low heat until chocolate melts; set aside to cool.

● Combine flour, the ¾ cup sugar, the baking powder, and ¼ teaspoon *salt* in a large mixing bowl; make a well in center. Add oil, egg yolks, the ⅓ cup cold water, and the vanilla. Beat with electric mixer on low to medium speed until combined. Beat on high speed about 3 minutes or until mixture is smooth. Beat in chocolate mixture on low speed; set aside.

● Thoroughly wash beaters. Place egg whites and cream of tartar in a very large mixing bowl; beat on medium to high speed until stiff peaks form (tips stand straight). Pour chocolate batter in a thin stream over egg white mixture and gently fold in.

● Pour batter into an ungreased 9x5x3-inch loaf pan. Bake in a 325° oven for 50 to 55 minutes or until top springs back when lightly touched. *Immediately* invert cake in pan. Cool completely. Loosen cake from pan. Remove cake from pan. Frost top and sides of cake with Mint Topping. Makes 8 servings.

Mint Topping: Beat together 1 cup *whipping cream,* 2 tablespoons *powdered sugar,* and 2 tablespoons *crème de menthe* or *crème de menthe syrup* in a medium bowl until stiff peaks form (tips stand straight).

Smooth Melting

Melting is the first step in many chocolate recipes. For best results, make sure your equipment is completely dry and be careful to keep water from splashing in the chocolate. Moisture can cause the chocolate to stiffen.

Speed the melting process by chopping chocolate blocks or squares into small pieces. Unsweetened chocolate liquefies when it melts; semisweet, sweet, and milk chocolates hold their shape when melted and should be stirred until smooth.

You may melt chocolate in a heavy saucepan over low heat. Stir constantly until chocolate begins to melt. Remove from heat and stir until smooth. If you use a double boiler, be sure the water in the lower pan doesn't boil or touch the top pan.

To melt chocolate in the microwave oven, place in a glass measure or custard cup. Cook, uncovered, on 100% power (high) until chocolate is almost melted. (Allow 1½ to 2½ minutes for 1 cup of chocolate pieces or two 1-ounce squares.) Remove from oven and stir until melted and smooth.

Macadamia Swirl Cheesecake

Per serving:
455 cal. (59% from fat), 8 g pro., 37 g carbo., 30 g fat,
118 mg cholesterol, 1 g dietary fiber, 224 mg sodium.

Preparation time:
20 minutes

Baking times:
8 minutes; 45 minutes

Cooling time:
2 hours 35 minutes

Chilling time:
4 hours

Only one word describes this chocolate-swirled, nut-crusted cheesecake—sublime! For a picture-perfect presentation, decorate the cheesecake with chocolate leaves, chocolate-dipped macadamia nuts, and a sprinkling of chopped macadamia nuts.

¾ cup all-purpose flour

3 tablespoons sugar

¼ cup margarine or butter

¼ cup finely chopped toasted macadamia nuts or almonds

1 egg white

¾ cup milk chocolate pieces

3 8-ounce packages cream cheese, softened

1 cup sugar

2 tablespoons all-purpose flour

2 eggs

1 egg yolk

¼ cup white crème de cacao or milk

Chocolate Leaves (see directions, page 9) (optional)

Chocolate-Dipped Macadamia Nuts (see directions, page 9) (optional)

● For crust, stir together the ¾ cup flour and the 3 tablespoons sugar. Cut in margarine until mixture is crumbly. Stir in chopped nuts and egg white. Pat *half* of the dough onto bottom of an 8- or 9-inch springform pan (with sides removed). Bake in a 375° oven for 8 to 10 minutes or until very light golden brown; cool on a wire rack. Butter sides of springform pan; attach sides to bottom. Pat remaining dough 1¾ inches up sides of 8-inch pan or 1½ inches up sides of 9-inch pan; set pan aside.

● For batter, melt chocolate pieces in a small heavy saucepan over very low heat, stirring constantly. Remove from heat. Beat cream cheese in large mixing bowl until fluffy. Stir together the 1 cup sugar and the 2 tablespoons flour; beat into cheese mixture. Add the 2 eggs and the egg yolk all at once, beating on low speed just until combined. *Do not overbeat.* Stir in crème de cacao or milk. Set aside *one-third* (about 1½ cups) of the batter. Stir melted chocolate into remaining batter.

● Spoon *half* of the chocolate batter into crust-lined pan. Carefully spoon *half* of the plain batter over the chocolate layer. Repeat layers. Carefully run a knife through the layers to swirl. Place springform pan on a shallow baking pan. Bake in a 375° oven for 45 to 50 minutes for 8-inch pan or 35 to 45 minutes for 9-inch pan, or until center appears nearly set when shaken.

● Cool on a wire rack for 5 minutes. Using a metal spatula, loosen crust from pan sides, leaving sides attached. Cool for 30 minutes more; remove pan sides. Cool 2 hours. Cover and chill at least 4 hours. To serve, transfer cheesecake (bottom of pan in place) to serving plate. Garnish with Chocolate Leaves and Chocolate-Dipped Macadamia Nuts, if desired. Makes 12 servings.

Macadamia Swirl Cheesecake

Almond-Chocolate Cheesecake

Per serving:
529 cal. (75% from fat), 10 g pro., 24 g carbo., 45 g fat,
131 mg cholesterol, 1 g dietary fiber, 279 mg sodium.

Preparation time:
20 minutes

Baking time:
45 minutes

Cooling time:
2 hours

Chilling time:
4 hours

Just when you thought cheesecake couldn't get any richer, we stirred chunks of milk chocolate with almonds into a white chocolate cheesecake. Toast the almonds for the crust before grinding to enhance their flavor (see tip, page 19).

2   teaspoons margarine or butter

¾   cup ground almonds

16   ounces white baking bar, chopped

4   8-ounce packages cream cheese, softened

½   cup margarine or butter, softened

3   tablespoons milk

1   tablespoon vanilla

Dash salt

4   eggs

1   egg yolk

4   1½-ounce bars milk chocolate with almonds, chopped

Chocolate Curls (see directions, page 9) (optional)

- Use the 2 teaspoons margarine to grease bottom and sides of a 10-inch springform pan. Press ground almonds onto bottom of springform pan. Set pan aside.

- For filling, heat and stir the white baking bar in a heavy medium saucepan over very low heat *just until melted.* Place melted baking bar, the cream cheese, the ½ cup margarine, the milk, vanilla, and salt in a large mixing bowl. Beat with an electric mixer on medium to high speed until well combined. Add whole eggs and egg yolk all at once. Beat on low speed *just until combined.* Stir in chopped milk chocolate.

- Pour filling into the prepared springform pan. Place springform pan on a shallow baking pan. Bake in a 375° oven for 45 to 50 minutes or until center appears nearly set when shaken.

- Cool cheesecake on a wire rack for 10 minutes. Using a small metal spatula, loosen cheesecake from pan sides, leaving sides attached. Cool for 30 minutes more; remove pan sides. Cool completely. Cover and chill at least 4 hours. Garnish with Chocolate Curls, if desired. Makes 16 servings.

White Chocolate: What's in a Name?

White baking bars and vanilla-flavored candy coating often are referred to as "white chocolate." But you won't find the words "white chocolate" on the label. These products lack chocolate solids, so they legally can't be labeled chocolate in the United States.

White baking bars melt much like chocolate and have a similar richness. Creamy white in color, they are flavored with sugar and vanilla.

Candy coating (sometimes called confectioner's coating or almond bark) is another chocolate-like product that contains no chocolate solids. Most or all of the cocoa butter has been replaced by other fat.

Cocoa-Berry Shortcakes

Per serving:
260 cal. (30% from fat), 6 g pro., 42 g carbo., 9 g fat,
3 mg cholesterol, 4 g dietary fiber, 133 mg sodium.

**Preparation time:
20 minutes**

**Baking time:
8 minutes**

Surprisingly low in calories and fat, these sumptuous shortcakes are filled with a honey-flavored banana cream. Another time, serve the filling as a dip for fresh fruit at a party.

1   cup all-purpose flour

¼   cup sugar

¼   cup unsweetened cocoa powder

1   teaspoon baking powder

3   tablespoons margarine or butter

⅔   cup milk

1   ripe large banana, peeled and cut into chunks

½   cup frozen whipped dessert topping, thawed

½   cup plain yogurt

1   teaspoon honey

     Dash ground nutmeg

3   cups fresh strawberries

- Lightly grease a baking sheet.

- For shortcakes, stir together flour, sugar, cocoa powder, and baking powder in a large bowl. Cut in margarine until mixture resembles coarse crumbs. Make a well in the center; add milk all at once. Stir just until dough clings together.

- Drop dough in 6 equal portions onto prepared baking sheet. Bake in a 450° oven for 8 to 10 minutes. Cool slightly on a wire rack.

- Meanwhile, for filling, mash banana with a fork until smooth. (You should have about ½ cup.) Add whipped topping, yogurt, honey, and nutmeg to mashed banana; stir until smooth. Reserve 6 whole strawberries for garnish; slice remaining berries.

- To assemble, split shortcakes in half crosswise. Set tops aside. Arrange strawberry slices on shortcake bottoms. Spoon *about 2 tablespoons* of the filling over sliced strawberries on *each* shortcake. Top with the shortcake tops. Spoon some of the remaining filling on top of each of the assembled shortcakes. Garnish with the reserved whole berries. Makes 6 servings.

Extra-Fudgey Hot Fudge Sauce

Whether you spoon it over a scoop of ice cream or drizzle it over a slice of pound cake, you're sure to enjoy this decadent hot fudge sauce. To prepare, combine one 6-ounce package *semisweet chocolate pieces*, one 5-ounce can (⅔ cup) *evaporated milk*, ¼ cup *light corn syrup*, and 1 tablespoon *margarine* or *butter* in a small heavy saucepan. Stir over low heat until the chocolate is melted. Stir in 1 teaspoon *vanilla*. Serve warm. Makes 1⅓ cups.

Duo-Chocolate Fondue

Individual Brownie Soufflés

Per serving:
418 cal. (53% from fat), 12 g pro., 39 g carbo., 26 g fat,
277 mg cholesterol, 1 g dietary fiber, 276 mg sodium.

Preparation time:
10 minutes

Baking time:
30 minutes

No need to spend time separating eggs for these streamlined soufflés. Just combine the ingredients in the blender or food processor and give them a whirl as directed in recipe.

4   eggs

⅓   cup milk

¼   cup granulated sugar

1   teaspoon vanilla

¼   teaspoon ground cinnamon

1   8-ounce package cream cheese, cut up

1   5½-ounce can (½ cup) chocolate-flavored syrup

2   teaspoons powdered sugar

- Combine eggs, milk, granulated sugar, vanilla, and cinnamon in a blender container or food processor bowl. Cover and blend or process until smooth. With blender or food processor running, add cream cheese pieces, blending until smooth.

- Add chocolate syrup. Cover and blend or process until combined. Pour mixture into four 1-cup soufflé dishes.

- Bake in a 375° oven for 30 to 35 minutes or until a knife inserted near the center comes out clean. *Quickly* sprinkle tops with powdered sugar. Serve immediately. Makes 4 servings.

Duo-Chocolate Fondue

Per serving:
448 cal. (55% from fat), 5 g pro., 47 g carbo., 29 g fat,
38 mg cholesterol, 4 g dietary fiber, 161 mg sodium.

Preparation time:
15 minutes

Dip your favorite fruits or pound cake into this mixture of semisweet and milk chocolate. Line the serving dishes with ground nuts, as shown opposite, for a crunchy accent.

2   teaspoons margarine or butter

¼   cup ground toasted walnuts or pecans

6   ounces semisweet chocolate, chopped

3   ounces milk chocolate, chopped

⅓   cup whipping cream

1   tablespoon margarine or butter

1   tablespoon amaretto or whipping cream

Pound cake cubes

Fresh strawberries, kiwi fruit chunks, papaya chunks, and/or Calimyrna (light) dried figs

- Use the 2 teaspoons margarine to grease six 4- to 6-ounce glass dessert dishes (such as sherbet dishes) or six individual soufflé dishes. Sprinkle the dessert dishes with the ground nuts to coat; set aside.

- For fondue mixture, combine semisweet chocolate, milk chocolate, the ⅓ cup whipping cream, the 1 tablespoon margarine, and the 1 tablespoon amaretto or cream in a heavy medium saucepan; heat and stir over low heat until chocolate is melted and mixture is smooth.

- To serve, carefully spoon fondue mixture into the nut-coated dessert dishes. Serve warm with pound cake and desired fruit. Makes 6 servings.

Chocolate Shortbread-Raspberry Torte

Per serving:
724 cal. (65% from fat), 6 g pro., 59 g carbo., 54 g fat, 108 mg cholesterol, 4 g dietary fiber, 219 mg sodium.

Preparation time:
40 minutes

Baking time:
20 minutes

Chilling times:
20 minutes; 2 hours

Our cover torte actually is a giant sandwich cookie! Layer homemade chocolate shortbread with whipped cream and raspberries. Be sure to chill the torte at least two hours for easier serving.

1	cup margarine or butter
¾	cup sugar
1	egg yolk
¾	cup finely chopped pecans
1½	cups all-purpose flour
⅓	cup unsweetened cocoa powder
¼	cup seedless raspberry jam
	Stabilized Whipped Cream (see tip, opposite)
2	cups fresh or frozen raspberries
	Melted white baking bar (optional)

- Bring margarine to room temperature; beat with an electric mixer for 30 seconds in a large mixing bowl. Add sugar; beat until combined. Beat in egg yolk and nuts. Stir together flour and cocoa powder in a medium mixing bowl. Gradually beat about *1 cup* of the flour mixture into margarine mixture just until combined. Stir in the remaining flour mixture. Divide dough into 4 equal portions; chill about 20 minutes.

- Remove one portion of dough from the refrigerator. Place this portion of dough on a baking sheet; cover with waxed paper and roll to form an 8-inch circle. Remove waxed paper and trim edges of dough with knife to make an even circle. Repeat with another portion of dough on a second baking sheet. Score *one* dough round into 8 wedges (do not cut all the way through dough).

- Bake in a 375° oven for 10 to 12 minutes or until firm. Cool on baking sheets for 5 minutes. Cut the scored shortbread into wedges. Cool all baked shortbread on wire racks. Let baking sheets cool completely, then repeat shaping and baking with the remaining 2 portions of dough, except *do not* score either portion. (Let dough stand at room temperature until easy to roll, if necessary.)

- Stir jam until softened. To assemble torte, place a whole shortbread round on a serving plate. Spread with *one-fourth* of the Stabilized Whipped Cream. Drizzle with *2 tablespoons* of the softened jam and arrange *½ cup* of the berries on top. Top with another whole shortbread round, another *one-fourth* of the Stabilized Whipped Cream, remaining preserves, and another *½ cup* of berries. Add remaining whole shortbread round.

- Spread remaining Stabilized Whipped Cream over top. Cover and chill 2 to 4 hours to soften the shortbread. Dip one edge of each shortbread wedge in melted white baking bar, if desired. Arrange shortbread wedges and remaining raspberries on top of torte. Cut into wedges with serrated knife. Makes 8 to 12 servings.

Note: Pictured on the cover.

Buttermilk-Chocolate Cake

Per serving:
526 cal. (35% from fat), 6 g pro., 83 g carbo., 22 g fat,
37 mg cholesterol, 2 g dietary fiber, 229 mg sodium.

Preparation time:
20 minutes

Baking time:
30 minutes

Cooling time:
1½ hours

This all-time-favorite cake boasts a rich, moist texture and a deep chocolate flavor. Frost with Chocolate-Buttermilk Frosting and embellish with your favorite chocolate garnish (see page 9).

2   cups all-purpose flour

1¾ cups granulated sugar

1   teaspoon baking powder

1   teaspoon baking soda

¼   teaspoon salt

1⅓ cups buttermilk

½   cup shortening

1   teaspoon vanilla

2   eggs

3   ounces unsweetened chocolate, melted and cooled

     Chocolate-Buttermilk Frosting (see recipe at right)

- Grease and lightly flour two 9x1½-inch round baking pans; set aside.

- Combine first 5 ingredients in a large mixing bowl. Add buttermilk, shortening, and vanilla. Beat with an electric mixer on low to medium speed about 30 seconds or until combined. Beat on medium to high speed for 2 minutes, scraping bowl occasionally. Add eggs and melted chocolate; beat 2 minutes more.

- Pour batter into prepared pans. Bake in a 350° oven for 30 to 35 minutes or until a wooden toothpick inserted near the centers comes out clean. Cool in pans on wire racks for 10 minutes. Remove cakes from pans; cool completely. Fill and frost with Chocolate-Buttermilk Frosting. Makes 12 servings.

Chocolate-Buttermilk Frosting: Beat ⅓ cup *margarine* or *butter* with an electric mixer on medium speed until fluffy. With mixer on low speed, slowly beat in 2 cups sifted *powdered sugar*. Slowly beat in 2 ounces *unsweetened chocolate* (melted and cooled), ¼ cup *buttermilk* or *milk*, and 1½ teaspoons *vanilla*. Slowly beat in 2 to 2½ cups sifted *powdered sugar* to make frosting of spreading consistency.

Stabilized Whipped Cream

Cakes frosted with whipped cream can get soggy as the whipped cream breaks down and becomes watery. For best results, whip the cream and assemble the cake no more than two hours before serving. Or, use stabilized whipped cream for cakes or desserts and assemble up to 24 hours before serving. Here's how to prepare stabilized whipped cream:

Combine 1 tablespoon *cold water* and ½ teaspoon *unflavored gelatin* in a 1-cup glass measure. Stir well; let stand 2 minutes. Then place measuring cup in pan of boiling water. Cook and stir about 1 minute or until gelatin is completely dissolved.

Place 2 cups *whipping cream*, ¼ cup *sugar*, and 2 teaspoons *vanilla* in a small mixing bowl. While beating the whipping cream mixture with an electric mixer on high speed, gradually drizzle the dissolved gelatin over it. Continue beating until stiff peaks form. Use immediately or store, covered, in the refrigerator for up to 48 hours. Makes 4 cups.

Chocolate-Hazelnut Torte

Per serving:
294 cal. (58% from fat), 4 g pro., 29 g carbo., 20 g fat,
53 mg cholesterol, 2 g dietary fiber, 121 mg sodium.

Preparation time:
15 minutes

Baking time:
40 minutes

Cooling time:
1½ hours

Chilling time:
4 hours

Standing time:
45 minutes

This dense, brownie-like dessert is double-drizzled with white and dark chocolate. Use extra hazelnuts as a garnish.

3 ounces unsweetened chocolate

¾ cup margarine or butter

1½ cups packed brown sugar

3 eggs

1 teaspoon vanilla

1 cup all-purpose flour

½ cup coarsely chopped hazelnuts (filberts)

- Grease and flour the bottom of an 8-inch springform pan; set aside.

- Combine unsweetened chocolate and margarine in a small heavy saucepan; heat over very low heat, stirring constantly until chocolate begins to melt. Immediately remove from heat and stir until smooth; cool slightly. Stir in brown sugar. Add eggs and vanilla. Lightly beat chocolate mixture by hand just until combined. (*Do not overbeat* or torte will rise during baking, then fall and crack.) Stir in flour. Spread chocolate mixture in prepared pan. Sprinkle with chopped hazelnuts.

- Bake in a 350° oven for 40 to 50 minutes or until a slight imprint remains when touched in the center of the torte. Let cool on a wire rack for 5 minutes. Using a knife, loosen torte from pan sides. Remove pan sides; cool completely. Chill in the refrigerator at least 4 hours.

- To serve, bring torte to room temperature. Warm a knife in hot water; dry thoroughly. Use knife to cut torte into wedges, rewarming knife as needed. Makes 12 servings.

Walnut Fudge Pudding Cake

Per serving:
380 cal. (45% from fat), 5 g pro., 49 g carbo., 20 g fat,
26 mg cholesterol, 2 g dietary fiber, 185 mg sodium.

Preparation time:
10 minutes

Baking time:
30 minutes

This dessert has remained popular over the years, and for good reason: The extra-moist cake makes its own fudge sauce as it bakes.

1 cup all-purpose flour

½ cup sugar

2 tablespoons unsweetened cocoa powder

2 teaspoons baking powder

½ cup half-and-half, light cream, or milk

2 tablespoons margarine or butter, melted

1 teaspoon vanilla

1 cup chopped walnuts

¾ cup sugar

¼ cup unsweetened cocoa powder

1½ cups boiling water

Whipped cream

- Stir together flour, the ½ cup sugar, the 2 tablespoons cocoa powder, the baking powder, and ¼ teaspoon *salt* in a large mixing bowl. Add half-and-half, melted margarine, and vanilla. Stir just until smooth. Stir in nuts. Spread in an ungreased 8x8x2-inch baking pan.

- Stir together the ¾ cup sugar and the ¼ cup cocoa powder in a medium mixing bowl. Stir in boiling water. Pour evenly over batter in pan. Bake in a 350° oven about 30 minutes or until a wooden toothpick inserted into top comes out clean. Serve warm with whipped cream. Makes 8 servings.

Chocolate-Hazelnut Torte

Chocolate Pots de Crème

Per serving:
271 cal. (64% from fat), 5 g pro., 22 g carbo., 21 g fat,
182 mg cholesterol, 1 g dietary fiber, 30 mg sodium.

Preparation time:
20 minutes

Chilling time:
2 hours

This classic French dessert (pronounced poh duh CREM) is so rich you'll want to serve it in small portions. Traditionally, tiny dessert cups with lids are called pots de crème cups.

1 cup half-and-half or light cream

1 4-ounce package sweet chocolate, coarsely chopped

2 teaspoons sugar

3 beaten egg yolks

½ teaspoon vanilla

Whipped cream (optional)

- Combine half-and-half, sweet chocolate, and sugar in a small heavy saucepan. Cook and stir over medium heat about 10 minutes or until mixture comes to a full boil and thickens.

- Gradually stir *about half* of the hot mixture into beaten egg yolks; return yolk mixture to saucepan. Cook and stir over low heat for 2 minutes more. Remove from heat. Stir in vanilla.

- Pour into 4 to 6 pots de crème cups or small dessert dishes. Cover and chill for 2 to 24 hours. Serve with whipped cream, if desired. Makes 4 to 6 servings.

Chocolate Bread Pudding

Per serving:
343 cal. (39% from fat), 8 g pro., 47 g carbo., 16 g fat,
98 mg cholesterol, 2 g dietary fiber, 165 mg sodium.

Preparation time:
15 minutes

Baking time:
40 minutes

Over the years, cooks have made bread pudding to use up stale bread. You won't want to wait for your bread to get stale to enjoy this chocolate-studded treat. To dry your own bread cubes, see page 52.

3 cups dry French bread cubes

2 cups milk

¾ cup sugar

¼ cup unsweetened cocoa powder

½ teaspoon ground cinnamon

2 eggs

1 tablespoon margarine or butter, melted

2 teaspoons vanilla

½ cup semisweet chocolate pieces

Whipped cream or vanilla or chocolate ice cream

- Combine bread cubes and milk in a large mixing bowl. Let stand for 10 to 15 minutes or until bread is softened, stirring once or twice.

- Meanwhile, stir together sugar, cocoa powder, and cinnamon in a small mixing bowl. Set aside. Using a rotary beater, beat together eggs, melted margarine, and vanilla in a medium mixing bowl. Add sugar mixture to egg mixture; beat until combined. Stir in semisweet chocolate pieces. Add the egg-sugar mixture to the bread mixture. Gently stir until mixtures are combined.

- Transfer bread-egg mixture to an ungreased 2-quart square baking dish. Bake in a 350° oven for 40 to 45 minutes or until a knife inserted near the center comes out clean. Serve warm with whipped cream or ice cream. Makes 6 to 8 servings.

Frothy Midnight Mocha

Per serving:
161 cal. (5% from fat), 12 g pro., 29 g carbo., 1 g fat,
6 mg cholesterol, 1 g dietary fiber, 162 mg sodium.

**Preparation time:
8 minutes**

Keep this spicy chocolate-and-coffee mix on hand for after-dinner or late-night sipping. Or, divide it among four Tupperware® Modular Mates® Round 2 containers and give as special gifts to friends.

2½ cups nonfat dry milk powder

1 cup sifted powdered sugar

½ cup unsweetened cocoa powder

¼ cup instant coffee crystals

½ teaspoon apple pie spice

- To make mocha mix, combine dry milk powder, powdered sugar, cocoa powder, coffee crystals, and apple pie spice in a Tupperware Oval 2 container or another airtight container. Seal and shake well to mix.

- *For each serving of mocha*, first stir the mix. Place ⅓ cup of the mix in a blender container or food processor bowl. Cover. With blender or processor running, add ⅔ cup *boiling water* through opening in lid or center feed tube. Blend or process until mixed and frothy. Makes 10 (6-ounce) servings.

Mexican Chocolate Floats

Per serving:
422 cal. (49% from fat), 11 g pro., 45 g carbo., 24 g fat,
76 mg cholesterol, 2 g dietary fiber, 161 mg sodium.

**Preparation time:
10 minutes**

**Chilling time:
3 hours**

Ground cinnamon is the secret ingredient in this foamy chocolate treat. Top it off with a scoop of chocolate or vanilla ice cream.

¼ cup sugar

¼ cup unsweetened cocoa powder

½ teaspoon ground cinnamon

2 cups milk

2 cups half-and-half or light cream

1 pint chocolate or vanilla ice cream (2 cups)

- Combine sugar, cocoa powder, and ground cinnamon in a large saucepan. Stir in milk. Cook and stir over low heat until sugar dissolves. Remove from heat. Stir in the half-and-half. Cover and chill.

- To serve, beat the chocolate mixture with a rotary beater until foamy. Place a scoop of ice cream in each of four Tupperware 12-oz. tumblers; fill with chocolate mixture. Makes 4 (12-ounce) servings.

Triple-Chocolate and Banana Malts

Per serving:
486 cal. (31% from fat), 10 g pro., 77 g carbo., 18 g fat,
54 mg cholesterol, 4 g dietary fiber, 215 mg sodium.

**Preparation time:
5 minutes**

This smooth sipper is perfect for summer. Use a blender or food processor to combine the ingredients just before serving.

1 cup chocolate-flavored or regular milk

2 tablespoons instant chocolate malted milk powder

1 ripe banana, cut up

1 pint chocolate ice cream (2 cups)

- Combine the milk and malted milk powder in a blender container. Cover and blend until the malted milk powder is dissolved. Add the cut-up banana and ice cream. Cover and blend until smooth. Pour into two Tupperware 12-oz. tumblers. Makes 2 (11-ounce) servings.

Fabulous
Finalés

So special, you want to savor them. So delicious, you want to devour them. That's what the recipes in this chapter have in common. Some, like this Summer Fruit Tart, can even double as a centerpiece. Turn the page and see for yourself—desserts don't get any more enticing than this.

Summer Fruit Tart
(See recipe, page 36.)

Summer Fruit Tart

Per serving:
296 cal. (38% from fat), 4 g pro., 44 g carbo., 13 g fat,
20 mg cholesterol, 2 g dietary fiber, 167 mg sodium.

Preparation time:
25 minutes

Baking time:
10 minutes

Cooling time:
30 minutes

Chilling time:
2 hours

This luscious dessert totes nicely in the Tupperware® 12" pie taker. Try it with other summer fruits, too, such as raspberries, pitted sweet cherries, nectarine slices, and kiwi fruit slices.

¾ cup all-purpose flour

1 tablespoon sugar

⅛ teaspoon salt

3 tablespoons margarine or butter, chilled

1½ to 2 tablespoons cold water

½ of an 8-ounce container soft-style cream cheese

2 tablespoons sugar

½ teaspoon vanilla

⅛ teaspoon ground nutmeg

6 strawberries, halved

2 small peaches, peeled, pitted, and sliced

2 plums, pitted and sliced

1 cup blueberries and/or boysenberries

⅓ cup apple jelly

1 ripe small banana

- For pastry, combine flour, the 1 tablespoon sugar, and the salt in a medium mixing bowl. Cut in margarine until pieces are the size of small peas. Sprinkle *1 tablespoon* of the cold water over part of mixture. Toss with fork. Push to side of the bowl. Repeat until all of the mixture is moistened. Form dough into a ball.

- Roll pastry into a 12-inch circle on lightly floured surface. Wrap pastry around rolling pin. Ease into a 10- or 11-inch tart pan. *Do not stretch pastry.* Press pastry ½ inch up sides of tart pan. If necessary, trim pastry even with top of pan. Prick bottom of pastry well with tines of a fork. Bake in a 450° oven for 10 to 12 minutes or until golden. Cool on a wire rack.

- Meanwhile, mix cream cheese, the 2 tablespoons sugar, the vanilla, and nutmeg until smooth. Spread in cooled crust. Arrange strawberries, peaches, plums, and blueberries and/or boysenberries over cheese mixture. Heat apple jelly in a small saucepan until melted. Spoon over fruit. Chill at least 2 hours.

- To serve, cut banana into diagonal slices; arrange sliced banana on tart. Makes 6 servings.

Note: Pictured on pages 34–35.

Lemon Champagne Sorbet

Per serving:
144 cal. (14% from fat), 1 g pro., 25 g carbo., 2 g fat,
7 mg cholesterol, 0 g dietary fiber, 34 mg sodium.

Preparation time:
15 minutes

Freezing time:
25 minutes (in ice cream freezer)

Made with champagne and half-and-half, this sorbet will remind you of sherbet. Serve scoops of this refreshing dessert in your prettiest wineglasses, and garnish with lemon peel strips.

½ cup sugar

1 envelope unflavored gelatin

1 cup water

⅔ cup light corn syrup

1 teaspoon finely shredded lemon peel

2 cups champagne or sparkling white grape juice

1 cup half-and-half or light cream

¼ cup lemon juice

Few drops yellow food coloring

- Combine sugar and unflavored gelatin in a medium saucepan. Add water and light corn syrup. Cook and stir over medium heat until sugar and gelatin dissolve. Remove from heat.

- Add lemon peel, champagne or sparkling white grape juice, half-and-half, lemon juice, and yellow food coloring. (Mixture will look curdled.)

- Freeze in a 4- to 5-quart ice cream freezer according to manufacturer's directions. (Or place in a 9x9x2-inch baking pan. Cover and freeze for 2 to 3 hours or until almost firm. Transfer mixture to a chilled bowl. Beat with an electric mixer until smooth but not melted. Return to baking pan. Cover and freeze until firm.) Makes 12 (½-cup) servings.

Fresh Raspberry Mousse

Per serving:
247 cal. (41% from fat), 3 g pro., 32 g carbo., 12 g fat,
41 mg cholesterol, 4 g dietary fiber, 16 mg sodium.

Preparation time:
15 minutes

Chilling times:
30 minutes; 2 hours

Welcome the arrival of summer with this exquisite mousse. Crown each dessert with "flowers" made from raspberries and mint leaves.

3 cups red raspberries

2 tablespoons raspberry liqueur or white grape juice

⅓ cup sugar

1 envelope unflavored gelatin

¾ cup boiling water

½ cup whipping cream

Red raspberries (optional)

Fresh mint (optional)

- For raspberry puree, combine the 3 cups raspberries and the raspberry liqueur or white grape juice in a blender container or food processor bowl. Cover and blend or process until smooth. Press mixture through a sieve to remove seeds; discard seeds. Set raspberry puree aside.

- Combine sugar and gelatin in a small mixing bowl; add the boiling water, stirring until gelatin dissolves. Transfer mixture to a medium mixing bowl. Stir in the raspberry puree. Cover and chill until mixture is partially set (the consistency of unbeaten egg whites), stirring several times.

- Beat whipping cream with an electric mixer on medium speed until soft peaks form. Fold whipped cream into partially set raspberry mixture. If necessary, chill again until the mixture mounds when spooned. Spoon into 4 wineglasses or dessert dishes. Cover and chill about 2 hours or until firm.

- To serve, garnish with additional raspberries and fresh mint, if desired. Makes 4 servings.

Berries, Melon, and Cream Sauce

Per serving:
263 cal. (35% from fat), 5 g pro., 40 g carbo., 11 g fat,
32 mg cholesterol, 5 g dietary fiber, 146 mg sodium.

Preparation time:
10 minutes

Enjoy raspberries and slices of honeydew with a dollop of this honey-flavored cream cheese. Or try cantaloupe and blueberries for another can't-miss combination.

½ cup soft-style cream cheese

½ cup vanilla yogurt

1 tablespoon honey

1 small honeydew melon, seeded, peeled, and cut into thin wedges

2 cups raspberries

- Combine cream cheese, vanilla yogurt, and honey in a small bowl. Serve immediately or cover and chill until serving time.

- To serve, arrange honeydew wedges in fan shapes on 4 individual dessert plates. Stir cream cheese mixture; spoon over melon. Top *each* serving with ½ *cup* of the raspberries. Cover and refrigerate any leftover topping. Makes 4 servings.

Praline-Filled Pumpkin
Cake Roll

Praline-Filled Pumpkin Cake Roll

Per serving:
401 cal. (50% from fat), 6 g pro., 46 g carbo., 23 g fat,
89 mg cholesterol, 2 g dietary fiber, 225 mg sodium.

Preparation time:
15 minutes

Baking time:
15 minutes

Cooling time:
1½ hours

Roll a tender pumpkin cake around a luscious, pecan-praline filling for a delectable holiday dessert. Just before serving, drizzle the cake roll with caramel ice cream topping and sprinkle with toasted chopped pecans, if you like.

3   eggs
1   cup granulated sugar
⅔   cup canned pumpkin
1   teaspoon lemon juice
¾   cup all-purpose flour
1½ teaspoons ground cinnamon
1   teaspoon baking powder
½   teaspoon salt
½   teaspoon ground ginger
½   teaspoon ground nutmeg
    Sifted powdered sugar
1   egg
⅔   cup packed brown sugar
1   5-ounce can (⅔ cup) evaporated milk
¼   cup margarine or butter
1½ cups toasted chopped pecans
1   4-ounce container frozen whipped dessert topping, thawed

● Grease and flour a 15x10x1-inch jelly-roll pan.

● Beat the 3 eggs with an electric mixer on high speed for 5 minutes or until thick and lemon colored. Gradually beat in the granulated sugar. Stir in pumpkin and lemon juice. Stir together flour, cinnamon, baking powder, salt, ginger, and nutmeg. Fold into pumpkin mixture. Spread in prepared jelly-roll pan.

● Bake in a 375° oven about 15 minutes or until cake springs back when lightly touched near center. *Immediately* loosen edges of cake from pan and turn cake out onto a towel sprinkled with powdered sugar. Roll up cake and towel jelly-roll style, starting from one of the cake's short sides. Cool completely on a wire rack.

● Meanwhile, for the praline filling, place the 1 egg in a small saucepan and beat just until mixed. Stir in brown sugar, evaporated milk, and margarine. Cook and stir over medium heat about 6 minutes or until thickened and bubbly. Stir in pecans. Cool thoroughly.

● Gently unroll the cake. Spread praline filling on cake to within ½ inch of the edges. Spread the whipped topping on top of the praline filling to within 1 inch of edges of cake. Roll up cake jelly-roll style, starting from one of the short sides. Transfer cake to a large serving platter. Makes 10 servings.

Cake Roll Success

For the best results, roll your cake while it's still warm. Otherwise the cake will crack. Using a towel coated with powdered sugar keeps the cake from sticking together as it cools. The powdered sugar also helps prevent the towel from sticking to the cake.

Pears with Chocolate Chips

Per serving:
152 cal. (20% from fat), 1 g pro., 33 g carbo., 4 g fat,
0 mg cholesterol, 6 g dietary fiber, 1 mg sodium.

Preparation time:
15 minutes

Baking time:
30 minutes

Preparing this classic combination is simple. Just sprinkle baked pears with mini chocolate chips— and enjoy!

4 medium pears

2 tablespoons lemon or lime juice

2 teaspoons vanilla

½ teaspoon ground cinnamon

¼ cup miniature semisweet chocolate pieces

- Core pears from bottom end, leaving stem intact. Using a vegetable peeler, such as the Tupperware® vegetable peeler, remove strips of peel at ½-inch intervals, starting at the top. If necessary, cut a thin slice from bottoms to help pears stand upright.

- Place pears on sides in a 2-quart square baking dish. Stir together lemon juice, vanilla, and cinnamon. Brush mixture onto pears. Pour any extra lemon juice mixture over pears.

- Bake, covered, in a 375° oven for 30 to 35 minutes or until pears are tender. Uncover; spoon any extra liquid over pears.

- To serve, place warm pears upright on dessert plates. Holding *each* pear by the stem and tipping slightly, sprinkle the sides of *each* pear with *1 tablespoon* chocolate pieces, turning the pear as you sprinkle. Serve warm. Makes 4 servings.

Baked Fruit Ambrosia

Per serving:
150 cal. (11% from fat), 1 g pro., 35 g carbo., 2 g fat,
0 mg cholesterol, 3 g dietary fiber, 7 mg sodium.

Preparation time:
15 minutes

Baking time:
15 minutes

A mélange of four fruits, this dessert is easy enough for everyday fare, yet elegant enough for company. Top with sour cream or whipped cream.

1 cup sliced peeled peaches or frozen unsweetened peach slices

1 8¾-ounce can unpeeled apricot halves, drained

1 cup seedless red grapes

1 cup cubed fresh pineapple or one 8¼-ounce can pineapple chunks, drained

¼ cup orange juice

2 tablespoons brown sugar

¼ teaspoon finely shredded lemon peel

1 tablespoon apricot brandy (optional)

¼ cup coconut

- Thaw peaches, if frozen. *Do not drain.* Combine the peaches and their juice, apricots, grapes, and pineapple in an ungreased 1½-quart casserole.

- Stir together orange juice, brown sugar, and lemon peel in a small mixing bowl. Stir in apricot brandy, if desired. Pour juice mixture evenly over fruit in casserole. Sprinkle fruit with coconut. Bake in a 425° oven about 15 minutes or until coconut is lightly browned. Serve warm. Makes 4 servings.

Pumpkin Cheesecake Squares

Per serving:
375 cal. (60% from fat), 7 g pro., 31 g carbo., 25 g fat,
128 mg cholesterol, 1 g dietary fiber, 278 mg sodium.

Preparation time:
20 minutes

Baking time:
40 minutes

Cooling time:
1½ hours

Chilling time:
4 hours

Move over pumpkin pie—and make room for this deliciously different holiday dessert. Use cinnamon-sugar to stencil a small pumpkin on the top of each square.

1	cup finely crushed graham crackers
2	tablespoons sugar
2	tablespoons margarine or butter, melted
1	8-ounce package cream cheese, softened
1	3-ounce package cream cheese, softened
½	cup sugar
1	cup canned pumpkin
1½	teaspoons pumpkin pie spice
½	teaspoon vanilla
3	eggs
¾	cup half-and-half, light cream, or milk
1	8-ounce carton dairy sour cream
1	tablespoon sugar

- For crust, stir together crushed graham crackers and the 2 tablespoons sugar in small mixing bowl. Stir in melted margarine. Press crumb mixture evenly onto bottom of 2-quart square baking dish. Set baking dish aside.

- For filling, beat cream cheese and the ½ cup sugar with an electric mixer on medium to high speed until well combined. Add pumpkin, pumpkin pie spice, vanilla, and ⅛ teaspoon *salt*. Beat until combined. Add eggs all at once. Beat mixture on low speed *just until combined*. Stir in half-and-half, light cream, or milk.

- Pour filling into the crust-lined baking dish. Bake in a 375° oven for 40 to 45 minutes or until the center is nearly set. Cool on a wire rack for 10 minutes.

- Meanwhile, combine sour cream and the 1 tablespoon sugar in a small mixing bowl. Spread over the cheesecake. Using a small metal spatula, loosen sides of cheesecake. Cool completely on a wire rack. Cover and chill for at least 4 hours before serving. Store in the refrigerator. Makes 9 servings.

Blueberry-Ricotta Squares

Per serving:
284 cal. (33% from fat), 8 g pro., 40 g carbo., 11 g fat,
82 mg cholesterol, 1 g dietary fiber, 173 mg sodium.

Preparation time:
15 minutes

Baking time:
55 minutes

Cooling time:
1½ hours

Bursting with blueberries, this cheesecake-topped dessert can double as a rich coffee cake. Arrange squares on your prettiest platter to serve.

1	cup all-purpose flour
¾	cup sugar
1¼	teaspoons baking powder
¼	teaspoon salt
⅓	cup milk
¼	cup shortening
1	egg
½	teaspoon vanilla
1½	cups blueberries
2	eggs
1¼	cups ricotta cheese
⅓	cup sugar
¼	teaspoon vanilla

- Grease a 9x9-inch baking pan.

- Combine flour, the ¾ cup sugar, the baking powder, and salt in a small mixing bowl. Add milk, shortening, the 1 egg, and the ½ teaspoon vanilla. Beat with an electric mixer on low speed until combined. Beat on medium speed for 1 minute more. Pour batter into prepared pan and spread evenly. Sprinkle blueberries over batter.

- Lightly beat the 2 eggs with a fork in a medium mixing bowl. Add ricotta cheese, the ⅓ cup sugar, and the ¼ teaspoon vanilla; beat until combined. Spoon ricotta mixture over blueberries and spread evenly.

- Bake in a 350° oven for 55 to 60 minutes or until knife inserted near center comes out clean. Cool completely on a wire rack. Serve immediately or cover and store in refrigerator. Makes 9 servings.

Strawberry-Rhubarb Lattice Pie

Per serving:
406 cal. (40% from fat), 5 g pro., 57 g carbo., 18 g fat,
27 mg cholesterol, 3 g dietary fiber, 144 mg sodium.

Preparation time:
25 minutes

Baking time:
40 minutes

Cooling time:
4 hours

Refrigerated piecrusts streamline the preparation of this popular pie. Turn to page 6 for tips on shaping the herringbone lattice crust. If you're pressed for time, use the instructions for the quick lattice crust as given in recipe.

2   cups fresh rhubarb cut into ½-inch pieces

2   tablespoons water

1   tablespoon lemon juice

1   cup sugar

¼   cup cornstarch

2   cups sliced fresh strawberries

½   to 1 teaspoon finely shredded lemon peel

Pastry for a 9-inch two-crust pie (see tips below and on page 44)

1   egg

1   teaspoon water

- For filling, stir together rhubarb, the 2 tablespoons water, and lemon juice in large saucepan. Bring to boiling. Reduce heat; simmer, covered, until liquid accumulates in saucepan. Stir together sugar and cornstarch; stir into rhubarb mixture in saucepan. Cook, stirring constantly, over medium heat until very thick. Stir in strawberries and lemon peel.

- Spoon filling into pastry-lined pie plate. Trim bottom crust to ½ inch beyond edge of pie plate. Cut top crust into ½- to ¾-inch strips with a pastry wheel or sharp knife. Gently lay *half* of the cut strips on top of filling, spacing at about 1-inch intervals.

- Place remaining pastry strips at right angles to the strips on filling. Trim the pastry strips even with bottom crust. Fold bottom pastry over lattice strips. Seal; flute edges.

- Beat together egg and the 1 teaspoon water in a small mixing bowl. Brush egg mixture over pastry. To prevent overbrowning, cover edge of pie with foil. Bake in 375° oven for 20 minutes. Remove foil. Bake for 20 to 25 minutes more or until golden and bubbly. Remove from oven. Cool pie on a wire rack. Makes 8 servings.

Pastry for Two-Crust Pie

Stir together 2 cups all-purpose *flour* and ½ teaspoon *salt* in a large mixing bowl. Using a pastry blender, cut in ⅔ cup *shortening* or *lard* until pieces are the size of small peas. Sprinkle 6 to 7 tablespoons *cold water*, 1 tablespoon at a time, over mixture, tossing with a fork after each addition until all is moistened. Divide dough in half. Form each half into a ball.

On a lightly floured surface slightly flatten one ball of dough with your hands. Roll dough from center to edges, forming a 12-inch circle. Wrap the pastry around the rolling pin. Unroll onto a 9-inch pie plate. Ease pastry into the pie plate, being careful not to stretch it. Repeat rolling for top crust. Continue as directed in the recipe.

Strawberry-Rhubarb Lattice Pie

Glazed Cherry Pie

Per serving:
454 cal. (35% from fat), 4 g pro., 71 g carbo., 18 g fat,
0 mg cholesterol, 3 g dietary fiber, 135 mg sodium.

Preparation time:
25 minutes

Baking time:
50 minutes

Cooling time:
4 hours

Cherry season or not, you can enjoy this special pie if you substitute frozen cherries for fresh cherries. When using frozen cherries, let them stand with the sugar and tapioca 60 minutes. Increase the baking time, also, to 50 minutes covered with foil and 20 to 30 minutes without the foil.

1¼ to 1½ cups granulated sugar

2 tablespoons quick-cooking tapioca

5 cups fresh pitted tart red cherries

Few drops almond extract

Pastry for a 9-inch two-crust pie (see tips, below and on page 42)

Cherry-Almond Glaze (see recipe at right)

- For filling, stir together granulated sugar and tapioca in a large mixing bowl. Add cherries and almond extract; gently toss until cherries are coated. Let stand about 15 minutes or until syrup forms, stirring occasionally.

- Stir filling; spoon into the pastry-lined pie plate. Trim crust even with edge of pie plate. Cut slits in the top crust. Place top crust on filling. Trim top crust ½ inch beyond edge of plate. Fold top crust under bottom pastry. Seal and flute edges. To prevent overbrowning, cover edge of pie with foil. Bake in a 375° oven for 25 minutes. Remove foil. Bake for 25 to 35 minutes more or until golden. Drizzle Cherry-Almond Glaze over hot pie. Cool pie on a wire rack. Makes 8 servings.

Cherry-Almond Glaze: Mix ¼ cup sifted *powdered sugar*, 1 teaspoon *cherry brandy* or *milk*, and ¼ teaspoon *almond extract* in a small mixing bowl. Stir in enough additional *cherry brandy* or *milk* (1 to 2 teaspoons) to make glaze of drizzling consistency.

Convenient Piecrust

Nothing is as tempting as a homemade pie, complete with a tender, flaky crust. If you don't have time to prepare pie pastry from scratch, try one of these easy options:

Frozen pastry shells: Choose regular or deep-dish pastry shells in foil pans. Most of the recipes in this cookbook will fill two regular or one deep-dish shell.

Folded refrigerated piecrusts: A 15-ounce package contains two 9-inch piecrusts. Use one piecrust for recipes calling for pastry for a one-crust pie. Use both piecrusts for recipes calling for pastry for a two-crust pie.

Piecrust sticks: Available in packages of two or four sticks, each piecrust stick can be combined with water and rolled into a 9-inch one-crust pie.

Piecrust mix: When combined with water, a package of piecrust mix will yield enough pastry for a 9-inch two-crust pie.

Honey-Almond Pie

Per serving:
604 cal. (51% from fat), 8 g pro., 67 g carbo., 35 g fat,
121 mg cholesterol, 2 g dietary fiber, 168 mg sodium.

Preparation time:
10 minutes

Baking times:
12 minutes; 45 minutes

Cooling time:
4 hours

First cousin to the pecan pie, this honey-of-a-pie tastes great topped with spoonfuls of almond-flavored whipped cream.

Pastry for a 9-inch one-crust pie (see tips, below and opposite)

3 eggs

¾ cup granulated sugar

¾ cup honey

⅓ cup margarine or butter, melted

1 tablespoon amaretto or ¼ teaspoon almond extract

1 cup sliced almonds, toasted

Flavored Whipped Cream (see recipe at right)

- Line piecrust with a double thickness of foil. Bake in a 450° oven for 8 minutes. Remove foil. Bake for 4 to 6 minutes more or until golden. Cool on a wire rack.

- Meanwhile, for filling, place eggs in a medium mixing bowl. Use a rotary beater or wire whisk to lightly beat eggs *just until mixed*. Stir in granulated sugar, honey, margarine, and amaretto or almond extract. Mix well. Stir in toasted almonds.

- Set pie plate on the oven rack; pour filling into the crust. To prevent overbrowning, cover edge of pie with foil. Bake in a 350° oven for 35 minutes. Remove foil. Bake for 10 to 15 minutes more or until a knife inserted near the center comes out clean. Cool on a wire rack.

- Serve pie with Flavored Whipped Cream. Cover and refrigerate to store. Makes 8 servings.

Flavored Whipped Cream: Chill a mixing bowl and the beaters of an electric mixer in the refrigerator. Combine 1 cup *whipping cream*, 2 tablespoons *powdered sugar*, 2 tablespoons *amaretto* or ½ teaspoon *almond extract*, and ½ teaspoon *vanilla* in chilled bowl. Using the chilled beaters, beat on medium speed of electric mixer until soft peaks form (tips curl).

Pastry for One-Crust Pie

Stir together 1¼ cups all-purpose *flour* and ¼ teaspoon *salt* in a medium mixing bowl. Using a pastry blender, cut in ⅓ cup *shortening* or *lard* until the pieces are the size of small peas. Sprinkle 3 to 4 tablespoons *cold water*, 1 tablespoon at a time, over mixture, tossing with a fork after each addition until all is moistened. Form dough into a ball.

Slightly flatten dough on a lightly floured surface. Roll dough from center to edges, forming a 12-inch circle. Wrap the pastry around the rolling pin. Unroll onto a 9-inch pie plate. Ease pastry into the pie plate, being careful not to stretch it.

Trim pastry to ½ inch beyond edge of plate. Fold under extra pastry. Crimp edge (see page 6). Continue as directed in recipes.

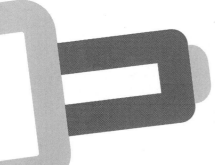

No-Peel Apple Pie

Per serving:
420 cal. (38% from fat), 4 g pro., 63 g carbo., 18 g fat,
0 mg cholesterol, 4 g dietary fiber, 135 mg sodium.

Preparation time:
20 minutes

Baking time:
1 hour

Cooling time:
1 hour

Choosing tender-skinned cooking apples is the secret to this no-peel apple pie. Opt for varieties such as Golden Delicious, Jonagold, or Jonathan.

6	large cooking apples
½	cup water
2	tablespoons lemon juice
½	cup sugar
2	tablespoons all-purpose flour
1½	teaspoons apple pie spice
	Pastry for a 9-inch two-crust pie (see tips, pages 42 and 44)
	Milk
	Sugar
	Whipped cream (optional)

● For filling, core and slice unpeeled apples (you should have 8 cups sliced apples). Combine apples, water, and lemon juice in a large mixing bowl; toss to coat. Stir together the ½ cup sugar, the flour, and apple pie spice in another large mixing bowl. Drain apples well; add apples to sugar mixture and toss gently to coat.

● Spoon filling into pastry-lined pie plate. Trim crust even with edge of pie plate.

● Cut a few small shapes from center of top crust; set shapes aside. Place top crust on filling. Trim top crust ½ inch beyond edge of pie plate. Fold top crust under bottom pastry. Seal and flute edges. Brush top crust with milk. Top with reserved cutouts, if desired; brush cutouts with milk. Sprinkle crust with sugar. To prevent overbrowning, cover edge of pie with foil.

● Bake in a 375° oven for 30 minutes. Remove foil. Bake about 30 minutes more or until golden. Cool on wire rack about 1 hour. Serve warm; top each serving with whipped cream, if desired. Makes 8 servings.

Apple-Cranberry Deep-Dish Pie

Per serving:
329 cal. (26% from fat), 3 g pro., 60 g carbo., 10 g fat,
27 mg cholesterol, 4 g dietary fiber, 83 mg sodium.

Preparation time:
25 minutes

Baking time:
50 minutes

Cooling time:
1 hour

Gussy up this home-style dessert with decorative pastry cutouts. Cut the pastry with cookie cutters and overlap the cutouts in place of the traditional top crust.

¼	cup sugar
3	tablespoons all-purpose flour
1	teaspoon apple pie spice or ¼ teaspoon ground nutmeg
1	teaspoon finely shredded orange peel
1½	cups canned whole cranberry sauce
7	cups peeled and thinly sliced cooking apples (about 2¼ pounds)
	Pastry for a 9-inch one-crust pie (see tips, pages 44 and 45)*
1	egg yolk
1	tablespoon water
1	tablespoon sugar

● For filling, stir together the ¼ cup sugar, the flour, apple pie spice or nutmeg, and orange peel in a mixing bowl. Stir in cranberry sauce. Add thinly sliced apples; toss to coat. Transfer apple mixture to a 10-inch deep-dish pie plate or a 1½-quart casserole.

● Place pastry on a lightly floured surface. Roll pastry from center to edges to make a 14-inch circle. Using cookie cutters, cut desired shapes from pastry, rerolling and cutting trimmings as necessary. Arrange cutouts on top of apple mixture, overlapping just the edges of the cutouts, so they bake evenly.

● Stir together egg yolk and water in a small bowl; brush onto pastry cutouts. Sprinkle with the 1 tablespoon sugar. Place pie plate or casserole on a baking sheet. Bake in a 375° oven for 50 to 55 minutes or until pastry is golden, apples are tender, and filling is bubbly. Cool on a wire rack about 1 hour. Use a spoon to serve warm. Makes 8 servings.

*Refer to directions in tip on page 45 for mixing dough only. Refer to directions above for rolling out dough.

Soda Fountain Pie

Per serving:
469 cal. (42% from fat), 6 g pro., 66 g carbo., 23 g fat,
30 mg cholesterol, 3 g dietary fiber, 244 mg sodium.

Preparation time:
20 minutes

Freezing times:
8 hours; 2 hours

Standing time:
30 minutes

Make your own strawberry ice cream using fresh strawberries and vanilla ice cream. Serve it in a sugar cone crust and smother with hot fudge sauce. Just before serving, garnish with whipped cream, if you like.

1½ cups crushed rolled sugar ice cream cones (one 5-ounce package or about 12 cones)

½ cup margarine or butter, melted

¼ cup sugar

3½ cups fresh strawberries

1 quart vanilla ice cream

⅓ cup vanilla malted milk powder

1 11¾-ounce jar hot fudge ice cream topping (about 1½ cups)

Whipped cream (optional)

- Combine crushed cones, margarine, and sugar in a small mixing bowl. Press onto the bottom and 1 inch up the sides of a 9-inch springform pan or into a 10-inch pie plate; set aside.

- For filling, place *3 cups* of the strawberries in a blender container. Cover; blend until smooth (should have about 1½ cups strawberry puree). Chop remaining strawberries. Place ice cream in a large chilled bowl; stir ice cream just to soften. Stir together chopped strawberries, strawberry puree, ice cream, and malted milk powder in a large mixing bowl. Pour into prepared crust. Cover; freeze 8 hours or until firm.

- Spread fudge ice cream topping over pie; freeze at least 2 hours more.

- To serve, let pie stand at room temperature for 30 minutes before cutting into wedges. Top each serving with whipped cream, if desired. Makes 10 servings.

Peanutty Ice Cream Pie

Per serving:
446 cal. (60% from fat), 12 g pro., 35 g carbo., 31 g fat,
29 mg cholesterol, 4 g dietary fiber, 271 mg sodium.

Preparation time:
25 minutes

Freezing time:
5 hours

Standing time:
10 minutes

Peanut butter lovers will adore this pie's crunchy crust and nutty-flavored filling. Make ahead and stash in the freezer in the Tupperware® 12" pie taker for a fast family dessert.

1½ cups coarsely ground peanuts

3 tablespoons margarine or butter, melted

2 tablespoons sugar

¼ cup flaked coconut

¼ cup light corn syrup

¼ cup peanut butter

3 tablespoons chopped peanuts

1 quart vanilla ice cream

Chopped candy-coated milk chocolate pieces (optional)

- Lightly grease a 9-inch pie plate. Combine the ground peanuts, the margarine, and sugar in a medium mixing bowl. Press mixture firmly onto bottom and up sides of the pie plate. Refrigerate for 15 minutes.

- Meanwhile, for filling, combine coconut, corn syrup, peanut butter, and the chopped peanuts in a small mixing bowl. Place ice cream in a large chilled bowl; stir ice cream just to soften. Stir in the peanut mixture just until combined. Spoon into chilled crust. Sprinkle chopped chocolate pieces over pie, if desired.

- Cover; freeze about 5 hours or until firm.

- To serve, let pie stand at room temperature for 10 minutes before cutting into wedges. Makes 8 servings.

Apricot-Apple Tarts

Apricot-Apple Tarts

Per serving:
462 cal. (24% from fat), 5 g pro., 75 g carbo., 13 g fat,
19 mg cholesterol, 4 g dietary fiber, 194 mg sodium.

Preparation time:
40 minutes

Baking time:
15 minutes

Cooking time:
30 minutes

The phyllo dough tart shells are easier than pie to prepare. Just layer the phyllo, brush with margarine, and cut into rectangles as directed at right. Make ahead and store in the Tupperware® Fresh-N-Fancy® container, if you like.

Margarine or butter

6   sheets frozen phyllo dough (18x14-inch rectangles), thawed

¼   cup margarine or butter, melted

1   6-ounce package dried apricots, snipped

1   cup water

½   cup light raisins

½   cup sugar

½   cup brandy or apple juice

1   tablespoon lemon juice

1½ cups chopped peeled cooking apples (2 medium)

1   tablespoon cornstarch

1   tablespoon cold water

Vanilla ice cream

Mint leaves (optional)

• Grease six 6-ounce custard cups with margarine so each cup is entirely covered. Set aside.

• Brush *one sheet* of phyllo dough with some of the melted margarine. (Remove one sheet of phyllo at a time and keep remaining sheets covered with a damp paper towel.) Top with another phyllo dough sheet; brush with some of the melted margarine. Repeat with remaining phyllo and melted margarine. Cut phyllo stack lengthwise into 6 strips; cut strips crosswise into thirds, forming 18 rectangles each 6 phyllo layers thick. Press *3 rectangles* evenly into *each* custard cup. Bake phyllo-lined cups in a 350° oven for 15 to 20 minutes or until golden. Remove phyllo shells from custard cups and cool completely on a wire rack.

• Combine apricots, the 1 cup water, the raisins, sugar, brandy or apple juice, and lemon juice in a saucepan. Bring to boiling; reduce heat. Simmer, uncovered, for 5 minutes. Stir in apples. Cook about 5 minutes more or until apples are tender, stirring occasionally. Stir together cornstarch and the 1 tablespoon cold water. Stir into apricot mixture. Cook and stir until thickened and bubbly. Cook and stir for 2 minutes more.

• To serve, spoon warm apricot mixture into baked phyllo shells. Top with ice cream. Garnish with mint, if desired. Makes 6 servings.

Pistachio-Almond Tarts

Per serving:
113 cal. (56% from fat), 2 g pro., 11 g carbo., 7 g fat,
13 mg cholesterol, 1 g dietary fiber, 46 mg sodium.

Preparation time:
25 minutes

Chilling time:
1 hour

Baking time:
25 minutes

Cooling time:
1 hour

Tassies with a twist! These tender cream cheese pastries are filled with a rich almond-paste mixture. Top with pistachios or with almonds.

½   cup margarine or butter

1   3-ounce package cream cheese

1   cup all-purpose flour

1   egg

½   cup sugar

½   of an 8-ounce can (½ cup) almond paste, crumbled

¼   cup coarsely chopped pistachios or almonds

• For crust, beat margarine and cream cheese with an electric mixer on medium to high speed about 30 seconds or until softened. Stir in flour. Cover and chill about 1 hour or until dough is easy to handle.

• Form chilled dough into a ball. Divide into 24 equal portions. Roll each portion into a ball. Place *each* ball into an ungreased 1¾-inch muffin cup. Press evenly against bottom and up sides of cup. Cover and set aside.

• For filling, beat egg, sugar, and almond paste in a small bowl until almost smooth. Stir in nuts. Fill *each* dough-lined muffin cup with a *rounded teaspoon* of filling.

• Bake in a 325° oven for 25 to 30 minutes or until tops are lightly browned. Cool slightly in pans. Remove tarts from pans and cool on wire racks. Makes 24 tarts.

Gingered Apple-Cranberry Crisp

Per serving:
401 cal. (41% from fat), 6 g pro., 56 g carbo., 19 g fat,
36 mg cholesterol, 5 g dietary fiber, 170 mg sodium.

Preparation time:
20 minutes

Baking time:
30 minutes

Cooling time:
30 minutes

Gingersnaps add flavor and crunch to this fabulous fall dessert. For a special touch, serve warm with a scoop of vanilla or cinnamon ice cream.

¾ cup rolled oats

¼ cup packed brown sugar

2 tablespoons all-purpose flour

⅓ cup margarine or butter

1 egg yolk

¾ cup coarsely crushed gingersnaps

½ cup chopped almonds or pecans

6 medium cooking apples, peeled, cored, and sliced (about 5½ cups)

1 cup cranberries, chopped

⅓ cup sugar

- For topping, stir together rolled oats, brown sugar, and flour in a medium mixing bowl.

- Cut in margarine until mixture resembles coarse crumbs. Add egg yolk; stir until combined. Stir in gingersnaps and almonds. Set topping aside.

- For filling, combine apples, cranberries, and sugar in a large mixing bowl. Toss until combined. Transfer filling to an ungreased 2-quart rectangular baking dish.

- Sprinkle the topping on the filling. Bake in a 375° oven for 30 to 35 minutes or until apples are tender (if necessary to prevent overbrowning, cover with foil the last 10 minutes of baking). Cool on wire rack about 30 minutes. Serve warm. Serves 6.

Rhubarb-Peach Betty

Per serving:
324 cal. (30% from fat), 3 g pro., 55 g carbo., 11 g fat,
1 mg cholesterol, 3 g dietary fiber, 296 mg sodium.

Preparation time:
35 minutes

Baking time:
25 minutes

Cooling time:
30 minutes

This mouthwatering dessert features a luscious fruit filling and crunchy bread cube topper. Serve it with half-and-half or light cream, if you like.

3 cups fresh or frozen unsweetened sliced rhubarb

2 cups sliced peeled peaches or frozen unsweetened peach slices

1 cup sugar

1 tablespoon all-purpose flour

¼ teaspoon salt

4 cups soft bread cubes (about 5 whole slices)

⅓ cup margarine or butter, melted

½ teaspoon finely shredded orange peel

- Thaw rhubarb and peaches, if frozen. *Do not drain.*

- For filling, combine sugar, flour, and salt in a large mixing bowl. Add rhubarb and peaches and their juice; gently toss until coated. Add *2 cups* of the bread cubes. Drizzle with *2 tablespoons* of the melted margarine; toss until mixed. Transfer fruit filling to an ungreased 2-quart square baking dish.

- For topping, combine the remaining bread cubes and the orange peel. Drizzle with the remaining melted margarine; toss until mixed. Sprinkle the topping over fruit filling.

- Bake in a 375° oven for 25 to 35 minutes or until fruit is tender and topping is golden brown. Cool on wire rack about 30 minutes. Serve warm. Makes 6 servings.

Caramel-Apple Bread Pudding

Per serving:
463 cal. (39% from fat), 10 g pro., 64 g carbo., 21 g fat, 162 mg cholesterol, 4 g dietary fiber, 281 mg sodium.

Preparation time:
15 minutes

Baking time:
40 minutes

Cooling time:
30 minutes

This apple-studded, caramel-sauced creation rivals even Grandma's bread pudding.

4   eggs

2¼ cups milk

½   cup granulated sugar

½   teaspoon ground cinnamon

½   teaspoon vanilla

⅛   teaspoon ground nutmeg

2   cups dry whole wheat bread cubes (about 3 whole slices)

1   6-ounce package dried apples, snipped

   Caramel-Nut Sauce (see recipe at right)

• Use a rotary beater to beat together eggs, milk, granulated sugar, cinnamon, vanilla, and nutmeg in a large mixing bowl. Set egg mixture aside.

• Toss together dry bread cubes and dried apples in an ungreased 8x1½-inch round baking pan. Pour the egg mixture evenly over the bread-apple mixture.

• Bake in a 350° oven for 40 to 45 minutes or until a knife inserted near the center comes out clean. Cool on wire rack about 30 minutes. Serve warm with Caramel-Nut Sauce. Makes 6 to 8 servings.

Caramel-Nut Sauce: Melt ¼ cup *margarine* or *butter* in a small saucepan. Stir in ½ cup packed *brown sugar* and 1 tablespoon *light corn syrup.* Cook and stir over medium heat until the mixture comes to a full boil. Stir in ¼ cup *whipping cream.* Return to a full boil. Remove from heat. Stir in ¼ cup chopped *pecans.* Serve warm.

Peach-Pineapple Crisp

Per serving:
390 cal. (46% from fat), 3 g pro., 51 g carbo., 20 g fat, 0 mg cholesterol, 2 g dietary fiber, 125 mg sodium.

Preparation time:
20 minutes

Baking time:
30 minutes

Cooling time:
30 minutes

Fresh peaches past their prime? Then use frozen slices. As a bonus, the macaroon and almond topping couldn't be any easier to prepare.

3   cups sliced peeled peaches or frozen unsweetened peach slices

1½ cups crumbled soft macaroon cookies (6 or 7 cookies)

¼   cup chopped almonds, toasted

3   tablespoons margarine or butter, melted

1   15¼-ounce can pineapple chunks, drained, or one 16-ounce can pear slices, drained

2   tablespoons sugar

2   tablespoons amaretto (optional)

• Thaw peaches, if frozen. *Do not drain.* For topping, stir together crumbled macaroons, chopped almonds, and melted margarine in a medium bowl. Set topping aside.

• For filling, stir together peaches and their juice, drained pineapple or pears, sugar, and, if desired, amaretto in a large mixing bowl. Transfer filling to an ungreased 1½-quart casserole.

• Sprinkle the topping on the filling. Bake in a 350° oven for 30 to 35 minutes or until the topping is golden. Cool on wire rack about 30 minutes. Serve warm. Serves 6.

Bread Pudding with Bourbon Sauce

Per serving:
561 cal. (44% from fat), 11 g pro., 66 g carbo., 28 g fat,
211 mg cholesterol, 2 g dietary fiber, 285 mg sodium.

Preparation time:
15 minutes

Baking time:
40 minutes

Cooling time:
30 minutes

Here's classic bread pudding at its best. For a contemporary flair, opt for the dried cranberries or cherries. You'll find them in the gourmet section of your grocery or at specialty food stores.

4   eggs

2¼ cups half-and-half or light cream

¾   cup sugar

1   tablespoon vanilla

4   cups dry French bread cubes

⅓   cup snipped dried apricots, light raisins, dried cranberries, or dried cherries

⅓   cup chopped pecans or walnuts

      Bourbon Sauce (see recipe at right)

- Use a rotary beater or wire whisk to lightly beat eggs in a large mixing bowl *just until mixed*. Stir in half-and-half or light cream, sugar, and vanilla. Set aside.

- Toss together bread cubes, dried apricots, and nuts in an ungreased 2-quart square baking dish. Pour the egg mixture evenly over the bread mixture.

- Bake in a 350° oven for 40 to 45 minutes or until a knife inserted near the center comes out clean. Cool on wire rack about 30 minutes. Serve warm with Bourbon Sauce. Makes 6 servings.

Bourbon Sauce: Melt ¼ cup *margarine* or *butter* in a small saucepan. Stir in ½ cup *sugar*, 1 beaten *egg yolk*, and 2 tablespoons *water*. Cook and stir over medium-low heat for 4 to 5 minutes or until sugar dissolves and mixture just begins to bubble. Remove from heat. Stir in 2 tablespoons *bourbon* or *apple juice*.

Bread Cube Basics

The key to great bread puddings is how you choose and handle the bread when making dry bread cubes. Here are some helpful hints:

Various breads absorb pudding differently, so it doesn't work to substitute one type of bread for another. For instance, don't use sliced white bread in a recipe that calls for French bread.

Take your choice: Either tear or cut the bread into ½-inch pieces or cubes.

You can oven-dry or air-dry the cubes. To oven-dry, spread the cubes in a single layer in a baking pan and bake in a 300° oven about 15 minutes or until the cubes are dry, stirring several times. To air-dry, spread the cubes in a single layer in a shallow baking pan and cover loosely with a thin towel. Let stand at room temperature for eight to 12 hours or until the cubes are dry.

Blackberry-Blueberry Cobbler Supreme

Per serving:
378 cal. (31% from fat), 5 g pro., 63 g carbo., 13 g fat,
21 mg cholesterol, 3 g dietary fiber, 207 mg sodium.

Preparation time:
15 minutes

Baking time:
40 minutes

Cooling time:
30 minutes

Frozen fruit works as well as fresh for this scrumptious cobbler. Just thaw the fruit and reserve the liquid. Then add enough grape or apple juice to the reserved liquid to make the 2 cups called for in the recipe.

1 cup all-purpose flour

1 cup whole wheat flour

2 teaspoons baking powder

¼ teaspoon salt

1 cup granulated sugar

½ cup margarine or butter, softened

¾ cup milk

2 cups fresh blackberries

1 cup fresh blueberries

½ to ¾ cup granulated sugar

2 cups grape or apple juice

Powdered sugar (optional)

Vanilla ice cream or light cream

- Grease a 13x9x2-inch baking pan or 3-quart rectangular baking dish.

- Stir together all-purpose flour, whole wheat flour, baking powder, and salt in a medium mixing bowl. Beat the 1 cup sugar and the margarine with an electric mixer until fluffy. Add flour mixture alternately with milk. Beat until smooth. Spread the batter evenly over the bottom of prepared baking pan or dish.

- Sprinkle blackberries and blueberries over batter, then sprinkle with the ½ to ¾ cup sugar, depending on the sweetness of fruit. Pour juice over fruit.

- Bake in a 350° oven for 40 to 45 minutes or until a wooden toothpick inserted in cake comes out clean. (Some of the fruit will sink toward the bottom as the cake rises to top.) Cool on wire rack about 30 minutes. Sprinkle lightly with powdered sugar, if desired. Serve warm with ice cream or light cream. Makes 12 servings.

White Cheesecake

Per serving:
450 cal. (71% from fat), 8 g pro., 25 g carbo., 36 g fat,
125 mg cholesterol, 1 g dietary fiber, 250 mg sodium.

Preparation time:
25 minutes

Baking times:
8 minutes; 40 minutes

Cooling time:
2 hours

Chilling time:
4 hours

The snowy white filling for this impressive cheesecake is minus the traditional egg yolks. To avoid cracks in the top of the cheesecake, beat the filling just until the ingredients are combined.

1 cup rolled oats

¾ cup all-purpose flour

¼ cup packed brown sugar

½ cup margarine or butter

2 beaten egg yolks

3 8-ounce packages cream cheese, softened

½ cup granulated sugar

2 tablespoons all-purpose flour

1 teaspoon vanilla

2 egg whites

1 cup whipping cream

- For crust, combine oats, the ¾ cup flour, and the brown sugar in a medium mixing bowl. Cut in margarine until crumbly. Set aside ¾ *cup* of the mixture for the topping. Stir egg yolks into the remaining mixture. Press onto the bottom and ½ inch up the sides of a 9-inch springform pan. Bake in a 375° oven for 8 minutes.

- For filling, combine softened cream cheese, granulated sugar, the 2 tablespoons flour, and the vanilla in a large mixing bowl. Beat with an electric mixer on medium speed until fluffy. Add egg whites all at once, beating on low speed *just until combined*. Stir in whipping cream. Pour filling into crust-lined pan. Sprinkle with reserved oat mixture.

- Place springform pan on a shallow baking pan. Bake in a 375° oven for 40 to 45 minutes or until center appears nearly set when shaken. Cool on a wire rack for 15 minutes. Using a metal spatula, loosen crust from pan sides. Cool for 30 minutes more; remove pan sides. Cool completely. Cover and chill at least 4 hours before serving. Makes 12 to 16 servings.

Marzipan Cheesecake

Per serving:
547 cal. (58% from fat), 11 g pro., 49 g carbo., 36 g fat,
144 mg cholesterol, 4 g dietary fiber, 320 mg sodium.

Preparation time:
25 minutes

Baking time:
1 hour

Cooling time:
2 hours

Chilling time:
4 hours

Cheesecakes don't get any better than this chocolate-crusted, cherry-sauced treat. The rich, almond-flavored filling is made with almond paste, which you can find in the baking section of your grocery store.

1½ cups finely crushed chocolate sandwich cookies (about 15 cookies)

3 tablespoons margarine or butter, melted

3 8-ounce packages cream cheese, softened

1 8-ounce can almond paste, crumbled

1 cup sugar

4 eggs

1 8-ounce carton dairy sour cream

Red Cherry Sauce (see recipe, below)

- For crust, grease a 9-inch springform pan. Combine crushed cookies and margarine in a small mixing bowl. Press onto the bottom of prepared pan. Set aside.

- For filling, place cream cheese and almond paste in a large mixing bowl. Beat with an electric mixer on medium-high speed until combined. Beat in sugar until fluffy. Add eggs and sour cream all at once, beating on low speed *just until combined*. Pour the filling into the crust-lined pan.

- Place springform pan on a shallow baking pan. Bake in a 325° oven about 1 hour or until center appears nearly set when shaken. Cool on a wire rack for 15 minutes. Using a metal spatula, loosen crust from pan sides. Cool for 30 minutes more; remove pan sides. Cool completely. Cover and chill at least 4 hours. Serve with Red Cherry Sauce. Makes 12 servings.

Red Cherry Sauce

Per serving:
47 cal. (2% from fat), 0 g pro., 12 g carbo., 0 g fat,
0 mg cholesterol, 0 g dietary fiber, 2 mg sodium.

Preparation time:
15 minutes

Don't stop with the Marzipan Cheesecake. Serve this distinctive sauce over vanilla ice cream or pound cake.

1½ cups frozen pitted tart red cherries or ½ cup dried cherries*

¼ cup packed brown sugar

2 tablespoons cornstarch

1 teaspoon finely shredded lemon peel

¼ teaspoon apple pie spice

1½ cups cranberry-cherry drink or unsweetened cherry juice*

- Stir together cherries, brown sugar, cornstarch, lemon peel, and apple pie spice in a small saucepan. Stir in cranberry-cherry drink.

- Cook and stir until thickened and bubbly. Cook and stir 2 minutes more. Serve warm. Makes about 2¼ cups.

*If using dried cherries, increase cranberry-cherry drink or cherry juice to 2 cups.

*Marzipan Cheesecake with
Red Cherry Sauce*

55

Very Berry Cheesecake

Per serving:
368 cal. (56% from fat), 8 g pro., 30 g carbo., 23 g fat,
105 mg cholesterol, 2 g dietary fiber, 293 mg sodium.

Preparation time:
25 minutes

Baking time:
40 minutes

Cooling time:
2 hours

Chilling time:
4 hours

For the ultimate blackberry cheesecake, use the blackberry options in the filling and in the topping.

6   tablespoons margarine or butter

1½ cups finely crushed vanilla wafers (about 40 wafers)

1   cup cream-style cottage cheese

2   8-ounce packages cream cheese, softened

¾   cup sugar

2   tablespoons all-purpose flour

2   teaspoons vanilla

¼   cup blackberry brandy or orange juice

3   eggs

1½ cups fresh raspberries, blueberries, and/or blackberries

     Berry Topping (see recipe at right)

- For crust, melt margarine in a small saucepan. Stir in crushed vanilla wafers. Spread mixture evenly into an 8-inch springform pan. Pat onto bottom and about 1¾ inches up the sides to form a firm, even crust.

- For filling, place cottage cheese in a blender container or food processor bowl. Cover and blend or process until cottage cheese is smooth.

- Place cream cheese, sugar, flour, and vanilla in a large mixing bowl. Beat with an electric mixer on medium to high speed until combined. Stir in blended cottage cheese and brandy or orange juice. Add eggs all at once. Beat on low speed *just until combined*.

- Pour about *half* of the filling into crust-lined pan. Sprinkle *1 cup* of the berries on top of the filling in pan. Spoon remaining filling over; top with remaining berries. Place springform pan on a shallow baking pan. Bake in a 375° oven for 40 to 45 minutes or until center appears nearly set when shaken.

- Cool on a wire rack for 15 minutes. Using a metal spatula, loosen crust from pan sides. Cool for 30 minutes more. Remove pan sides. Cool completely. Cover and chill at least 4 hours.

- To serve, slice and top with Berry Topping. Serves 12.

Berry Topping: Toss together 2 cups fresh *raspberries, blueberries,* and/or *blackberries*; 1 tablespoon *sugar*; and 1 tablespoon *blackberry brandy* or *orange juice* in a medium mixing bowl. Cover and chill until serving time.

Checking Cheesecake for Doneness

What's the most difficult part of preparing a cheesecake? Deciding when it's done! Here's how we recommend you check for doneness:

Gently shake the cheesecake. The center should appear nearly set. A 1-inch area in the center will jiggle slightly when the cheesecake is done (this area will firm as it cools). Don't use a knife to test the doneness of cheesecake because the knife will make a crack.

Pumpkin-Pear Upside-Down Cake

Per serving:
368 cal. (37% from fat), 4 g pro., 56 g carbo., 16 g fat,
0 mg cholesterol, 2 g dietary fiber, 1,294 mg sodium.

Preparation time:
20 minutes

Baking time:
50 minutes

Cooling time:
5 minutes

When you turn this pumpkin cake upside down, you'll find a luscious layer of caramelized pears. Serve warm with a dollop of whipped cream, if you like.

²⁄₃ cup packed brown sugar

¼ cup margarine or butter, melted

1 teaspoon cornstarch

1 16-ounce can pear halves in light syrup

1½ cups all-purpose flour

1½ teaspoons pumpkin pie spice

1 teaspoon baking soda

¾ teaspoon baking powder

4 egg whites

1 cup sugar

1 cup canned pumpkin

½ cup cooking oil

• Combine brown sugar, melted margarine, and cornstarch in a small mixing bowl. Drain pears, reserving *3 tablespoons* of the syrup. Stir reserved syrup into brown sugar mixture. Pour mixture into a 10-inch round baking pan or a 9x9x2-inch baking pan. (If desired, form pears into fans by cutting 3 or 4 lengthwise slits ½ inch from the top of pear to the bottom.) Arrange pear halves, small ends toward the center and rounded sides down, on top of the mixture in pan.

• Combine flour, pumpkin pie spice, baking soda, and baking powder in a medium mixing bowl; set aside. Place egg whites in large mixing bowl. Beat with electric mixer on medium speed until soft peaks form. Gradually add sugar, beating until stiff peaks form (tips stand straight). Using low speed, mix in pumpkin and oil. Fold in flour mixture just until moistened. Carefully spoon over pears; spread evenly with back of a spoon. Bake in a 350° oven for 50 to 60 minutes or until a wooden toothpick inserted near center comes out clean. Cool about 5 minutes. Loosen from pan sides; invert onto serving plate. Serve warm. Makes 10 to 12 servings.

Cranberry-Apple Cake

Per serving:
404 cal. (34% from fat), 4 g pro., 61 g carbo., 15 g fat,
36 mg cholesterol, 3 g dietary fiber, 172 mg sodium.

Preparation time:
20 minutes

Baking time:
40 minutes

Cooling time:
30 minutes

Serve this crumb-topped cake while it's still warm with sour cream or whipping cream. If you must make it ahead, reheat in a 350° oven for five to 10 minutes or until warm.

1¼ cups all-purpose flour

2 tablespoons sugar

1 teaspoon baking powder

⅓ cup margarine

1 egg yolk

2 tablespoons brandy or milk

2 cups sliced peeled apples

1 cup cranberries

¾ cup sugar

¼ cup rolled oats

2 tablespoons all-purpose flour

½ teaspoon ground cinnamon

2 tablespoons margarine

• Stir together the 1¼ cups flour, the 2 tablespoons sugar, the baking powder, and ¼ teaspoon *salt* in a medium mixing bowl. Cut in the ⅓ cup margarine until mixture resembles coarse crumbs. Combine egg yolk and brandy or milk; add to dry ingredients and mix well. Press mixture onto bottom and up sides of a 9x1½-inch round baking pan. Arrange apple slices over crust. Sprinkle with cranberries.

• Combine the ¾ cup sugar, the oats, the 2 tablespoons flour, and the cinnamon in a medium mixing bowl. Cut in the 2 tablespoons margarine until mixture resembles coarse crumbs. Sprinkle over apples and cranberries.

• Bake in a 350° oven for 40 to 45 minutes or until apples are tender. Cool on wire rack about 30 minutes. Serve warm. Makes 6 to 8 servings.

Orange-Laced Carrot Cake

Orange-Laced Carrot Cake

Per serving:
713 cal. (43% from fat), 6 g pro., 98 g carbo., 34 g fat,
92 mg cholesterol, 2 g dietary fiber, 252 mg sodium.

Preparation time:
30 minutes

Baking time:
30 minutes

Cooling time:
1½ hours

Assembling time:
15 minutes

A cake this delicious should look as good as it tastes. Spread the top layer of the carrot cake with orange marmalade, then pipe the Orange Frosting in a lattice design, using a decorating bag and a small star tip.

2	cups all-purpose flour
2	cups granulated sugar
1	teaspoon baking powder
1	teaspoon baking soda
1	teaspoon ground cinnamon
3	cups finely shredded carrot
1	cup cooking oil
4	eggs
2	teaspoons finely shredded orange peel
	Orange Frosting (see recipe at right)
⅓	cup orange marmalade

● Grease and lightly flour two 9x1½-inch round baking pans. Set pans aside.

● Stir together flour, granulated sugar, baking powder, baking soda, and cinnamon in mixing bowl. Add carrot, oil, eggs, and orange peel. Beat with an electric mixer on low to medium speed until ingredients are combined.

● Spread batter in the prepared pans. Bake in a 350° oven for 30 to 35 minutes or until a wooden toothpick inserted near the centers of the cakes comes out clean. Cool cakes in pans on wire racks for 10 minutes. Remove cakes; cool completely on racks.

● To assemble, place first cake layer on a large serving plate. Spread with some of the Orange Frosting. Top with the remaining cake layer. Spread orange marmalade over top. Frost the sides of the cake with some more of the frosting. Spoon the remaining frosting into a decorating bag fitted with a small star tip (about ¼-inch opening). Pipe a lattice design over marmalade. Pipe 2 lines around lattice. Serve immediately or cover and store in the refrigerator. Makes 12 servings.

Orange Frosting: Place one 8-ounce package *cream cheese*, ½ cup *margarine* or *butter*, and 2 teaspoons finely shredded *orange peel* in a large mixing bowl. Beat with an electric mixer on medium speed until fluffy. Gradually add 2½ cups sifted *powdered sugar*, beating well. Gradually beat in 2¼ to 2½ cups sifted *powdered sugar* to make frosting of spreading consistency.

Bake-Ahead Cakes

Get a head start on cake preparation by baking the cake layers and storing them in the freezer until you're ready to frost. Place the cake layers, separated by waxed paper, in the Tupperware® 10" cake taker. Or, freeze the layers individually in freezer bags. Unfrosted cake layers freeze well for up to six months. To thaw, remove the layers from the Cake Taker or freezer bags and let stand loosely covered at room temperature for a few hours.

Pineapple-Coconut Carrot Cake

Per serving:
691 cal. (43% from fat), 6 g pro., 94 g carbo., 34 g fat,
87 mg cholesterol, 2 g dietary fiber, 234 mg sodium.

Preparation time:
30 minutes

Baking time:
35 minutes

Cooling time:
1½ hours

You'll have a hard time finding a carrot cake any moister than this! Stir in ½ cup chopped walnuts, if you want to add some extra crunch.

2	cups all-purpose flour
2	cups granulated sugar
1	teaspoon baking powder
1	teaspoon baking soda
1	teaspoon ground cinnamon
3	cups finely shredded carrot
1	8¼-ounce can crushed pineapple
1	cup cooking oil
½	cup coconut
4	eggs
	Cream Cheese Frosting (see recipe at right)

- Grease and flour two 9x1½-inch round baking pans.

- Stir together flour, granulated sugar, baking powder, baking soda, and cinnamon in a large mixing bowl. Add carrot, *undrained* pineapple, oil, coconut, and eggs. Beat with an electric mixer on low to medium speed until ingredients are combined.

- Spread batter in prepared pans. Bake in a 350° oven about 35 minutes or until a wooden toothpick inserted near centers of cakes comes out clean. Cool in pans on wire racks for 10 minutes. Remove from pans; cool completely. Frost with Cream Cheese Frosting. Serve immediately or cover and store in refrigerator. Serves 12.

Cream Cheese Frosting: Place two 3-ounce packages *cream cheese*, ½ cup softened *margarine* or *butter*, and 2 teaspoons *vanilla* in a large mixing bowl. Beat with an electric mixer on medium speed until light and fluffy. Gradually add 2 cups sifted *powdered sugar*, beating well. Gradually beat in 2½ to 2¾ cups sifted *powdered sugar* to make frosting of spreading consistency.

Coconut Cream Flan

Per serving:
347 cal. (51% from fat), 7 g pro., 36 g carbo., 20 g fat,
168 mg cholesterol, 2 g dietary fiber, 74 mg sodium.

Preparation time:
15 minutes

Baking time:
50 minutes

Cooling time:
1 hour

Chilling time:
4 hours

Toasted coconut and almonds dress up this classic, caramel-coated custard. For smoothest texture, be careful not to overbeat the eggs.

½	cup sugar
4	eggs
1¾	cups half-and-half, light cream, or milk
⅓	cup sugar
⅓	cup cream of coconut
¼	teaspoon almond extract
¾	cup flaked coconut, toasted
2	tablespoons sliced almonds, toasted

- To caramelize sugar, place the ½ cup sugar in heavy 8-inch skillet; heat over medium-high heat (*do not stir*) until sugar begins to melt, shaking skillet occasionally. Reduce heat to low. Cook about 5 minutes more or until a golden liquid, stirring frequently. Remove from heat and *immediately* pour into 8x1½-inch round baking pan. Quickly rotate pan to coat bottom and sides evenly.

- Use a rotary beater or wire whisk to lightly beat eggs in a large mixing bowl *just until mixed*. Stir in half-and-half, the ⅓ cup sugar, the cream of coconut, and almond extract. Fold in *½ cup* of the toasted coconut.

- Place caramel-coated pan in a 13x9x2-inch baking pan; set on the oven rack. Pour egg mixture into caramel-coated pan. Pour *boiling or hottest tap water* into the 13x9x2-inch pan to a depth of 1 inch. Bake in a 325° oven for 50 to 55 minutes or until a knife inserted near the center comes out clean. Remove pan with flan from water. Cool on a wire rack. Cover; chill at least 4 hours.

- To serve, unmold flan onto a serving plate with sides. Top with any sugar that remains in pan. Sprinkle with remaining coconut and the almonds. Serves 6 to 8.

Candy Bar Raspberry Torte

Per serving:
610 cal. (49% from fat), 7 g pro., 72 g carbo., 34 g fat, 114 mg cholesterol, 1 g dietary fiber, 265 mg sodium.

Preparation time:
50 minutes

Baking time:
30 minutes

Cooling time:
1½ hours

Finish the sides of this white chocolate torte with a decorating comb. Make wavy or straight lines as you pull the comb gently around the cake.

3 2.2-ounce creamy white candy bars with almonds

½ cup water

2¼ cups sifted cake flour or 2 cups all-purpose flour

2 teaspoons baking powder

¼ teaspoon baking soda

1 cup margarine or butter

1½ cups granulated sugar

4 egg yolks

1 cup buttermilk

4 egg whites

¼ cup granulated sugar

1 10- or 12-ounce jar seedless raspberry jam

Whipped Cream Frosting (see recipe at right)

- Grease and flour three 9x1½-inch round baking pans. Set aside *half* of one candy bar. Break up remaining bars; combine with the water in small saucepan. Heat and stir over low heat until melted. Cool 20 minutes.

- Combine flour, baking powder, and baking soda. Beat margarine with electric mixer on medium speed for 30 seconds. Add the 1½ cups sugar; beat until fluffy. Beat in egg yolks, then melted candy. Alternately add flour mixture and buttermilk, beating after each addition.

- Thoroughly wash beaters. Beat whites in large bowl until soft peaks form (tips curl). Gradually add the ¼ cup sugar, beating until stiff peaks form (tips stand straight). Fold into batter. Divide evenly among prepared pans.

- Bake in a 350° oven about 30 minutes or until a wooden toothpick inserted in centers comes out clean. Cool on wire racks 10 minutes. Remove from pans; cool.

- To serve, spread jam between layers. Spread Whipped Cream Frosting over top and sides. Shave reserved candy on top. Makes 12 servings.

Whipped Cream Frosting: Beat together 1½ cups *whipping cream*, ¼ cup sifted *powdered sugar*, and ½ teaspoon *vanilla* until soft peaks form (tips curl).

Wonderful Whipped Cream

No matter how you prefer it—with or without sugar and flavorings—whipped cream is a wonderful way to garnish your favorite desserts. Because cream whips best when very cold, we recommend chilling the mixing bowl and beaters in the refrigerator about 15 minutes before whipping.

For 1 cup of sweetened whipped cream, combine ½ cup *whipping cream*, 1 tablespoon *powdered sugar*, and ¼ teaspoon *vanilla* in a chilled bowl. Beat with chilled beaters on low speed until soft peaks form.

For 1 cup flavored whipped cream, prepare sweetened whipped cream as directed above, *except* beat in one of the following flavorings: 1 tablespoon *unsweetened cocoa powder* plus 2 teaspoons *sugar*, 1 tablespoon *liqueur*, ¼ teaspoon *almond extract*, ¼ teaspoon finely shredded *citrus peel*, or ⅛ teaspoon ground *cinnamon*.

Time-Minded
Temptations

No matter how busy your schedule, you'll always have time for the desserts in this chapter. That's because each is made from six or fewer ingredients. Next time you want to give yourself a break, give Lemon Mousse Torte—or any of the other spectacular treats you'll find here—a try.

Lemon Mousse Torte
(See recipe, page 64.)

Lemon Mousse Torte

Per serving:
253 cal. (30% from fat), 3 g pro., 41 g carbo., 9 g fat,
30 mg cholesterol, 0 g dietary fiber, 414 mg sodium.

Preparation time:
20 minutes

Baking time:
30 minutes

Cooling time:
1½ hours

Chilling time:
2 hours

Take advantage of convenient cake and pudding mixes to create this tempting torte. Crown it with twists of sliced lemon and a mint leaf.

1 package 1-layer-size yellow cake mix

1 egg

1 4-serving-size package instant lemon pudding mix

1 cup cold milk

1 4-ounce container frozen whipped dessert topping, thawed

- Prepare yellow cake mix according to package directions using the egg. Bake in a 9x1½-inch round baking pan according to package directions. Cool on a wire rack for 10 minutes. Remove from pan. Cool completely on wire rack. Cut cake in half horizontally to make 2 layers. Set cake layers aside.

- For mousse, combine lemon pudding mix and milk in a large mixing bowl. Beat with an electric mixer on low speed until combined. Beat on high speed for 2 to 3 minutes or until mixture is thick. Fold in *half* of the dessert topping.

- Place bottom cake layer, cut side up, on a serving plate. Spread with about *half* of the mousse. Place top cake layer, cut side down, on top of mousse layer. Spread remaining mousse on top cake layer. Spread remaining dessert topping on sides.

- Cover and chill torte for 2 to 3 hours. Makes 8 servings.

Note: Pictured on pages 62–63.

Chocolate Fluff

Per serving:
219 cal. (43% from fat), 3 g pro., 27 g carbo., 11 g fat,
19 mg cholesterol, 0 g dietary fiber, 156 mg sodium.

Preparation time:
10 minutes

Here's a quick fix-up for purchased pound cake, angel cake, or fresh fruit. Combine chocolate pudding with whipped topping and liqueur. Then just spoon it on!

½ cup canned or prepared chocolate pudding, chilled

1 tablespoon crème de cacao, coffee liqueur, white crème de menthe, or milk

1 4-ounce container frozen whipped dessert topping, thawed

Pound cake, angel cake, or fresh fruit

- Stir together chocolate pudding and liqueur or milk in a medium mixing bowl. Fold in dessert topping.

- Spoon mixture over pound cake, angel cake, or fresh fruit. Makes 6 servings.

Vanilla Fluff: Prepare Chocolate Fluff as directed, *except* substitute vanilla pudding for chocolate pudding and orange liqueur or orange juice for the liqueur or milk called for in main recipe. (The nutrition information per serving is the same as above *except:* 216 cal., 174 mg sodium.)

Mocha Mousse

Per serving:
124 cal. (27% from fat), 3 g pro., 21 g carbo., 4 g fat,
5 mg cholesterol, 0 g dietary fiber, 273 mg sodium.

**Preparation time:
10 minutes**

Transform chocolate pudding mix into something special with instant coffee crystals and dessert topping mix.

1½ cups milk

2 teaspoons instant coffee crystals

1 4-serving-size package instant chocolate pudding mix

1 4-ounce container frozen whipped dessert topping, thawed

- Combine milk and coffee crystals in a small mixing bowl. Let stand 5 minutes to dissolve crystals.

- Stir pudding mix into the coffee mixture. Beat with an electric mixer on low speed about 30 seconds or until moistened. Beat on high speed about 2 minutes more or until very well blended. Fold in dessert topping.

- Spoon mixture into 6 individual dessert dishes. Serve immediately or chill until serving time. Serves 6.

Strawberry Daiquiri Dessert

Per serving:
142 cal. (44% from fat), 1 g pro., 16 g carbo., 7 g fat,
0 mg cholesterol, 1 g dietary fiber, 8 mg sodium.

**Preparation time:
10 minutes**

Fold puréed strawberries and rum into whipped topping for this almost-instant dessert.

1 10-ounce package frozen strawberries

¼ cup light rum or apple juice

2 tablespoons lemon juice

1 8-ounce container frozen whipped dessert topping, thawed

- Partially thaw and break up frozen strawberries; combine with light rum or apple juice and lemon juice in a blender container or food processor bowl. Cover; blend or process until thoroughly mixed.

- Transfer strawberry mixture to a medium mixing bowl. Fold in whipped dessert topping.

- Spoon mixture into 8 chilled sherbet dishes or stemmed glasses. Serve immediately. Makes 8 servings.

Homemade Cakes in Half the Time!

You can prepare a homemade cake in a hurry when you start with a two-layer yellow, white, or chocolate cake mix and customize it as follows:

For spiced cakes, with the dry cake mix stir in ¾ teaspoon *ground cinnamon or ginger,* ½ teaspoon *ground allspice,* or ¼ teaspoon *ground nutmeg.*

For flavored cakes, with the eggs stir in ½ cup *applesauce,* 1 tablespoon *instant coffee crystals* (dissolved in water called for in mix directions), 1 tablespoon finely shredded *orange peel,* 1 teaspoon *maple flavoring,* or ½ teaspoon *almond extract.*

For tempting bits and pieces, into the mixed batter stir in 1 cup *flaked coconut,* ½ cup finely chopped *nuts,* ½ cup *miniature semisweet chocolate pieces,* or ½ cup well-drained chopped *maraschino cherries.*

Double-Chocolate Ice Cream

Per serving:
312 cal. (60% from fat), 3 g pro., 29 g carbo., 22 g fat,
72 mg cholesterol, 1 g dietary fiber, 63 mg sodium.

Preparation time:
15 minutes

Freezing time:
6 hours

Imagine—homemade ice cream that rivals premium brands for creaminess and flavor. You don't even need an ice cream maker to prepare it.

2 cups whipping cream

½ of a 14-ounce can (⅔ cup) sweetened condensed milk

⅔ cup chocolate-flavored syrup

½ cup miniature semisweet chocolate pieces

- Combine whipping cream, sweetened condensed milk, and chocolate syrup in a large mixing bowl. Beat with an electric mixer on medium to high speed about 10 minutes or until soft peaks form (tips curl). Fold in chocolate pieces.

- Transfer to an 8x8x2-inch baking pan. Cover and freeze for at least 6 hours or until firm.

- Scoop the ice cream into sherbet or dessert dishes. Makes 10 to 12 servings.

Peaches and Cream Tart

Per serving:
316 cal. (50% from fat), 6 g pro., 35 g carbo., 18 g fat,
17 mg cholesterol, 1 g dietary fiber, 316 mg sodium.

Preparation time:
15 minutes

Baking time:
15 minutes

Cooling time:
45 minutes

Thanks to frozen puff pastry, this pretty-as-a-picture tart is a cinch to prepare. Embellish the tart with decorative leaves cut from the extra strip of puff pastry.

½ of a 17¼-ounce package frozen puff pastry, thawed (1 sheet)

1½ cups canned or prepared vanilla pudding, chilled

½ cup dairy sour cream

1 teaspoon finely shredded orange peel or few drops almond extract

2 to 3 cups frozen unsweetened peach slices and/or blueberries, slightly thawed

- Roll pastry into a 12-inch square. Cut four 12x1-inch strips of dough off one side of the pastry square. Cut *one* of the 12x1-inch strips in half crosswise. Transfer rectangle to an ungreased baking sheet. Using a fork, prick pastry at 1-inch intervals. Brush edges of rectangle with *water.*

- Lay *one* 12x1-inch strip on *each* of the long sides of rectangle to form sides. Place *one* 6x1-inch strip on *each* short end. Cut remaining 12x1-inch strip into decorative shapes. Bake pastry shell and decorative shapes in a 375° oven about 15 minutes or until golden. Cool on a wire rack. Transfer to a serving plate.

- For filling, stir together pudding, sour cream, and shredded orange peel or almond extract. Spoon into pastry shell. Arrange peaches and/or blueberries on top of pudding. Garnish with decorative pastry shapes. Makes 6 servings.

Peaches and Cream Tart

67

Pound Cake Torte

Per serving:
166 cal. (36% from fat), 3 g pro., 25 g carbo., 7 g fat,
19 mg cholesterol, 1 g dietary fiber, 140 mg sodium.

Preparation time:
15 minutes

For a special effect, buy the ice cream topping in a plastic squeeze bottle and drizzle an attractive design on top of the pound cake.

1   cup thinly sliced strawberries or chopped peaches

½   cup strawberry or peach yogurt

1   10¾-ounce frozen loaf pound cake

¼   cup chocolate fudge ice cream topping

- Fold strawberries or peaches into the strawberry or peach yogurt. Set aside.

- Slice the frozen pound cake lengthwise into 3 layers. Spread the fruit-yogurt mixture between the cake layers. Spread the ice cream topping over the top layer. Serve immediately or cover and chill until serving time. Makes 10 servings.

Glazed Pound Cake

Per serving:
213 cal. (29% from fat), 2 g pro., 37 g carbo., 7 g fat,
22 mg cholesterol, 2 g dietary fiber, 166 mg sodium.

Preparation time:
10 minutes

To make this quick dessert company-special, spoon whipped cream over each slice. Guests will love it!

2   cups fresh or frozen raspberries

1   10¾-ounce frozen loaf pound cake, thawed

¼   cup raspberry syrup

3   tablespoons seedless red raspberry preserves

- If using frozen raspberries, thaw slightly. Before removing cake from the cake pan, prick the cake all over the top with a long-tined fork. Slowly spoon raspberry syrup over pound cake, directing the syrup into the holes. Spread with raspberry preserves.

- Serve immediately or cover and chill for 3 to 24 hours. To serve, slice cake and spoon raspberries over slices. Makes 8 to 10 servings.

Black Forest Torte

Per serving:
399 cal. (33% from fat), 4 g pro., 64 g carbo., 15 g fat,
21 mg cholesterol, 1 g dietary fiber, 247 mg sodium.

Preparation time:
25 minutes

Baking time:
30 minutes

Cooling time:
1½ hours

Bake refrigerated brownie dough in cake pans and layer with cherry pie filling for the easiest Black Forest "torte" ever. Another time, substitute apricot pie filling for the cherry.

1   19.8-ounce package fudge brownie mix

1   egg

⅓   cup cooking oil

1   21-ounce can cherry pie filling

¼   cup sliced almonds, toasted

- Grease two 8x1½-inch round baking pans. Prepare brownie mix according to package directions using egg and oil. Spread *half* of the dough over bottom of *each* prepared pan. Bake in a 350° oven about 30 minutes or until edges are firm. Cool in pans on wire racks for 10 minutes. Remove from pans. Cool completely.

- Place one brownie layer on a serving plate. Set aside ½ *cup* pie filling. Spoon remaining pie filling over brownie layer. Place the second brownie layer on top of filling. Top with reserved pie filling. Sprinkle with almonds. Makes 10 to 12 servings.

Cream Cheese-Filled Pastries

Per serving:
110 cal. (49% from fat), 2 g pro., 13 g carbo., 6 g fat,
0 mg cholesterol, 1 g dietary fiber, 136 mg sodium.

Preparation time:
20 minutes

Baking time:
10 minutes

Cooling time:
30 minutes

Make this elegant dessert ahead and freeze in the Tupperware® Freezer Mates® Medium 2 container. Just before serving, trim with additional toasted almonds.

1   11-ounce package piecrust mix

½   cup sugar

¼   cup unsweetened cocoa powder

6   tablespoons cold water

1   8-ounce carton soft-style cream cheese with strawberries

- Combine piecrust mix, sugar, and cocoa powder in a medium mixing bowl. Mix well.

- Gradually add cold water, tossing with a fork until dough forms a ball. Divide dough in half.

- On floured surface, roll each half of dough into a 12x8-inch rectangle. Cut into 2-inch squares; use a fork to prick each in a decorative design. Transfer pastry squares to 2 baking sheets. Bake in a 375° oven about 10 minutes or just until set. Remove to wire racks and let cool.

- To assemble pastries, spread cream cheese onto *half* of the pastry squares, using about 1 teaspoon cream cheese for each square. Top with remaining squares, pressing together lightly. Makes 24 pastries.

Mississippi Mud Sundaes

Per serving:
335 cal. (38% from fat), 7 g pro., 48 g carbo., 15 g fat,
36 mg cholesterol, 2 g dietary fiber, 131 mg sodium.

Preparation time:
10 minutes

Chocoholics will want to keep their cupboards stocked with the four ingredients for this rich peanut butter-and-chocolate sauce. Besides ice cream, the sauce is also delicious over pound cake or angel cake.

¾   cup sugar

⅓   cup unsweetened cocoa powder

1   5-ounce can (⅔ cup) evaporated milk

¼   cup chunky peanut butter

1½ cups vanilla or chocolate ice cream

- Stir together sugar and cocoa powder in a small saucepan. Stir in evaporated milk.

- Cook and stir over medium-high heat until mixture is boiling. Remove from heat. Stir in chunky peanut butter until smooth.

- Serve warm sauce over scoops of vanilla or chocolate ice cream. Makes 6 servings.

Microwave Cooking Directions: Stir together sugar and cocoa powder in a small microwave-safe mixing bowl. Stir in evaporated milk. Micro-cook, uncovered, on 100% power (high) for 2 to 3 minutes or until mixture is boiling, stirring once. Stir in chunky peanut butter until smooth. Serve as directed above.

Caramel-Pear Crisp

Caramel-Pear Crisp

Per serving:
466 cal. (36% from fat), 6 g pro., 73 g carbo., 20 g fat, 29 mg cholesterol, 7 g dietary fiber, 271 mg sodium.

Preparation time:
15 minutes

Baking time:
30 minutes

Cooling time:
30 minutes

Prepare this old-fashioned dessert the modern no-fuss way. Toss pears with caramel ice cream topping for the filling, then sprinkle with the quick crumb topping made of crushed gingersnaps, crushed granola, and margarine.

¾ cup crushed gingersnaps

¾ cup coarsely crushed granola

¼ cup margarine or butter, melted

6 or 7 medium pears

⅓ cup caramel or butterscotch ice cream topping

Vanilla ice cream or whipped cream (optional)

- Combine gingersnaps, granola, and melted margarine in a medium mixing bowl. Set aside.

- Peel, core, and slice pears. Measure 6 cups sliced fruit. Arrange fruit in an even layer in a 2-quart rectangular baking dish. Drizzle ice cream topping over fruit. Sprinkle gingersnap mixture over fruit.

- Bake, uncovered, in a 350° oven for 30 to 35 minutes or until fruit is tender when tested with a fork. Cool on wire rack for 30 minutes. Serve warm; top with vanilla ice cream or whipped cream, if desired. Makes 6 servings.

Cheesy Lemon Pudding

Per serving:
154 cal. (23% from fat), 6 g pro., 24 g carbo., 4 g fat, 15 mg cholesterol, 0 g dietary fiber, 346 mg sodium.

Preparation time:
15 minutes

Make an ordinary meal extraordinary with this layered pudding. Stir lemonade concentrate into ricotta cheese for the luscious lemon layer.

1 cup ricotta cheese

2 tablespoons frozen lemonade concentrate

1 4-serving-size package instant vanilla pudding mix

Ground nutmeg

- Combine ricotta cheese and lemonade concentrate in a small mixing bowl. Set aside. Prepare vanilla pudding according to package directions.

- Divide *half* of the pudding among 5 dessert dishes. Top with ricotta mixture. Pour remaining pudding on top of ricotta mixture in the dishes. Sprinkle lightly with nutmeg. Makes 5 servings.

Whipped Cream on Call

Love whipped cream but hate the last-minute hassle? Whip it up ahead of time (see directions for making whipped cream on page 61), then spoon or pipe individual servings onto a waxed-paper-lined baking sheet. Place the baking sheet in the freezer and freeze the whipped cream until firm. Transfer the whipped cream mounds to a freezer container such as a Tupperware® Freezer Mates® container and store in the freezer.

To serve, place a mound of frozen whipped cream on each serving of dessert and let servings stand at room temperature about 20 minutes or until the whipped cream thaws.

Apple Crunch

Per serving:
114 cal. (14% from fat), 1 g pro., 25 g carbo., 2 g fat,
0 mg cholesterol, 3 g dietary fiber, 21 mg sodium.

Preparation time:
10 minutes

Baking time:
40 minutes

Firm, tart apples usually
are best for baking. Good
choices include Golden
Delicious, Granny Smith,
Jonathan, Jonagold, and
Winesap.

3	medium cooking apples (1 pound total)
¼	cup apple or orange juice
1	tablespoon brown sugar
1	teaspoon cornstarch
⅓	cup granola

- Peel, core, and thinly slice apples. Combine apple juice, brown sugar, and cornstarch. Toss with apples. Place apple mixture in a 1-quart casserole.

- Cover and bake in a 350° oven for 40 to 45 minutes or until apples are very tender. Sprinkle granola over apple mixture; serve warm. Makes 4 servings.

Chocolate-Peanut Butter Pudding Cake

Per serving:
297 cal. (28% from fat), 6 g pro., 53 g carbo., 10 g fat,
24 mg cholesterol, 2 g dietary fiber, 344 mg sodium.

Preparation time:
15 minutes

Baking time:
40 minutes

Cooling time:
30 minutes

Chocolate syrup, peanut
butter, and peanuts turn a
convenient cake mix into
an irresistible double-
chocolate pudding cake.

1	16-ounce can chocolate-flavored syrup
2	tablespoons peanut butter
1	package 1-layer-size devil's food or dark fudge cake mix
1	egg
½	cup chopped peanuts

- Combine chocolate syrup, peanut butter, and ¼ cup *water* in a small saucepan; heat and stir until smooth. Set aside.

- Prepare cake mix according to package directions using the egg. Stir in chopped peanuts. Transfer the cake batter to an ungreased 2-quart casserole. Drizzle the chocolate syrup mixture evenly over the cake batter.

- Bake in a 350° oven about 40 minutes or until a wooden toothpick inserted into the top comes out clean. Cool on wire rack for 30 minutes. Serve warm. Makes 9 servings.

Gorp 'n' Spice Cupcakes

Per serving:
148 cal. (35% from fat), 2 g pro., 23 g carbo., 6 g fat,
18 mg cholesterol, 1 g dietary fiber, 148 mg sodium.

Preparation time:
10 minutes

Baking time:
20 minutes

Cooling time:
1 hour

If you can't find spice cake
mix, substitute white or
yellow mix and stir in 1
teaspoon ground cinnamon.

1	package 1-layer-size spice cake mix
1	egg
⅓	cup mixed dried fruit bits
⅓	cup miniature semisweet chocolate pieces
¼	cup chopped pecans

- Line muffin cups with paper bake cups. Set aside. Prepare cake mix according to package directions using the egg, *except use only ⅓ cup water.* Stir in fruit bits.

- Fill each muffin cup ⅔ full. Sprinkle chocolate pieces and chopped pecans over batter. Bake in a 350° oven about 20 minutes or until a wooden toothpick inserted in the centers comes out clean. Cool on wire racks. Makes 12 cupcakes.

Fresh Fruit Fix-Ups

It's hard to find an easier—or more delicious—dessert than fresh fruit. Pick from these sensational and simple ideas.

Fruited Angel Torte: Slice a purchased *angel cake* in half horizontally to make two layers. Combine 4 cups sliced *fresh fruit* and 2 cups *sweetened whipped cream* or frozen *whipped dessert topping,* thawed. Spread *half* of the fruit mixture over the bottom cake layer. Add the other cake layer, then top with the remaining fruit mixture. Chill torte at least 2 hours before serving. Makes 12 servings.
Per serving: 226 cal. (31% from fat), 4 g pro., 36 g carbo., 8 g fat, 27 mg cholesterol, 2 g dietary fiber, 405 mg sodium.

Fruit and Cream Cheese Bites: Spread or pipe about 1 teaspoon purchased *flavored cream cheese* onto a *rich round cracker.* Arrange fresh *fruit pieces* on top of crackers. Use colorful fruits, such as kiwi fruit, strawberries, grapes, blueberries, mandarin oranges, pineapple, or cantaloupe, honeydew, or other melon.
Per cracker: 33 cal. (62% from fat), 1 g pro., 3 g carbo., 2 g fat, 0 mg cholesterol, 0 g dietary fiber, 52 mg sodium.

Sparkling Fruit Sippers: Spoon chunks of *fresh fruit* or whole *berries* into long-stemmed wineglasses. Cover fruit with *sparkling mineral water* or *champagne.*
Per 6-ounce serving: 63 cal. (1% from fat), 0 g pro., 16 g carbo., 0 g fat, 0 mg cholesterol, 1 g dietary fiber, 7 mg sodium.

Grilled Rum Bananas: Slit unpeeled *bananas* lengthwise, cutting to, but not through the opposite side; open slightly. Grill over *medium* coals or broil 5 to 6 inches from heat until skins darken and bananas soften. Let diners season their own bananas with *rum, brandy,* a *flavored liqueur, brown* or *powdered sugar,* or *lemon* or *lime wedges.*
Per banana: 174 cal. (3% from fat), 1 g pro., 27 g carbo., 1 g fat, 0 mg cholesterol, 2 g dietary fiber, 1 mg sodium.

Broiled Fruit Desserts: Place quarters of ripe fresh *pineapple* or halves of fresh *pears, apples, grapefruit,* or peeled *peaches,* cut side up, on an unheated broiler pan. Sprinkle fruit with *brown sugar.* Broil 5 to 6 inches from heat for 3 to 5 minutes or until warm and sugar melts. Dot with *margarine* or *butter,* if desired.
Per pineapple quarter: 91 cal. (5% from fat), 0 g pro., 23 g carbo., 1 g fat, 0 mg cholesterol, 1 g dietary fiber, 5 mg sodium.

Watermelon Fruit Bowl: Remove pulp from a *watermelon* half, being careful to keep the rind intact. Cut points or scallops along edge of rind, if desired. Cut pulp into cubes. Return melon cubes to watermelon "bowl." Add other fruits, such as *cantaloupe* or other *melon, grapes,* or *strawberries.* Pour chilled *white wine, fruit-flavored wine,* or *lemon-lime carbonated beverage* over fruit just before serving.
Per ½-cup serving: 51 cal. (6% from fat), 0 g pro., 8 g carbo., 0 g fat, 0 mg cholesterol, 1 g dietary fiber, 3 mg sodium.

Chocolate-Dipped Fruit: Dip whole *strawberries, orange sections,* or wedges of fresh *pears, apples,* or *nectarines* in melted *white baking bar* or *semisweet chocolate.* Cover only half of the fruit to allow colors to show. Place on a foil-lined baking sheet and freeze 2 to 3 minutes to harden baking bar or chocolate. Refrigerate dipped fruit until ready to serve. (Hint: Dip fruits that will discolor, such as apples, pears, and nectarines, in lemon juice and pat dry with paper towels before dipping in baking bar or chocolate.)
Per strawberry: 81 cal. (57% from fat), 1 g pro., 8 g carbo., 5 g fat, 0 mg cholesterol, 0 g dietary fiber, 13 mg sodium.

Mock Crème Brûlée: Place 3 cups fresh *fruit slices* or *chunks,* or whole straw*berries* in a broiler-proof pan. Spoon ⅓ cup dairy *sour cream* or plain *yogurt* over fruit and sprinkle with 3 tablespoons *brown sugar.* Broil 5 to 6 inches from heat for 3 to 5 minutes or until brown sugar melts. Makes 4 to 6 servings.
Per serving: 121 cal. (29% from fat), 1 g pro., 22 g carbo., 4 g fat, 8 mg cholesterol, 2 g dietary fiber, 13 mg sodium.

Fruit Kabobs: Make kabobs using a variety of *fruit chunks,* whole *strawberries,* or seedless *grapes.* Serve fruit kabobs with canned or prepared *vanilla pudding* or *flavored yogurt* as a dip. Use scooped-out halved *grapefruits, cantaloupes, honeydews,* or *oranges* for pudding containers, if desired.
Per kabob: 70 cal. (18% from fat), 1 g pro., 14 g carbo., 2 g fat, 0 mg cholesterol, 1 g dietary fiber, 76 mg sodium.

Slimsational
Sweet Treats

Imagine desserts so light even the strictest dieter can indulge. Treat yourself to Raspberry Crepes, Mocha Soufflé, the individual meringues shown here, or any of the recipes in this section. You'll soon discover that you can satisfy your sweet tooth whenever you want—always with a maximum of flavor and a minimum of fat and calories.

Summer Fruit in Individual
Meringues (See recipe, page 76.)

Summer Fruit in Individual Meringues

Per serving:
185 cal. (2% from fat), 4 g pro., 44 g carbo., 0 g fat,
1 mg cholesterol, 2 g dietary fiber, 44 mg sodium.

Preparation time:
1 hour

Baking time:
35 minutes

Cooling time:
1 hour

For perfect meringues every time you serve these tangy orange-sauced desserts, check the tip opposite. Or, look for ready-made meringues in the bakery sections of larger supermarkets.

3	egg whites
1	teaspoon vanilla
¼	teaspoon cream of tartar
1	cup sugar
½	teaspoon finely shredded orange peel
½	cup orange juice
¼	cup cold water
2	teaspoons cornstarch
1	teaspoon honey
1	8-ounce carton plain nonfat yogurt or nonfat sour cream
2	tablespoons lower-calorie orange marmalade
2	kiwi fruit, peeled and sliced
2	plums, pitted and cut into wedges
1½	cups blueberries and/or raspberries
2	small oranges, peeled and sectioned

- Let egg whites stand at room temperature in a small mixing bowl for 30 minutes. Cover a baking sheet with plain brown paper. Draw eight 3½-inch circles 2 inches apart on brown paper. Set aside.

- Add vanilla and cream of tartar to egg whites. Beat with an electric mixer on medium speed until soft peaks form (tips curl). Add sugar, 1 tablespoon at a time, beating on high speed until stiff peaks form (tips stand straight) and sugar is almost dissolved.

- Spread about *2 teaspoons* of the meringue mixture to form a 2½-inch-diameter circle in the center of *each* circle on the paper. Using a pastry bag fitted with a large star tip (½-inch opening), pipe remaining meringue around the circles, building the sides up to form shells. (Or, use a spoon to spread mixture over each circle, building sides higher than the center to form shells.)

- Bake in 300° oven for 35 minutes. Turn off oven and let shells cool and dry in oven with door closed for 1 hour.

- Meanwhile, for sauce, stir together orange peel, orange juice, water, and cornstarch in a small saucepan. Cook and stir over medium heat until mixture is thickened and bubbly. Cook and stir 2 minutes more. Stir in honey. Cover and chill thoroughly.

- To assemble individual meringue shells, stir together yogurt or sour cream and marmalade. Divide mixture among the shells. Combine the kiwi fruit, plums, berries, and oranges. Divide fruit among the shells. Drizzle orange sauce over the fruit. Makes 8 servings.

Note: Pictured on pages 74–75.

Apricots with Raspberry Topper

Per serving:
104 cal. (7% from fat), 2 g pro., 24 g carbo., 1 g fat,
1 mg cholesterol, 2 g dietary fiber, 21 mg sodium.

Preparation time:
15 minutes

Toss raspberries with your choice of lemon, pineapple, or vanilla yogurt for a luscious low-fat topping. Another time, try the topping on canned peach halves or pineapple slices.

½	of an 8-ounce carton lemon, pineapple, or vanilla low-fat yogurt
½	cup fresh or loose-pack frozen raspberries
1	16-ounce can unpeeled apricot halves in light syrup, drained
1	tablespoon coconut or sliced almonds, toasted

- Combine yogurt and raspberries in a small mixing bowl. Set mixture aside.

- Cut each apricot half in half again. Divide apricots among 4 dessert dishes. Spoon yogurt mixture over apricots in dessert dishes. Sprinkle with toasted coconut or almonds. Makes 4 servings.

Chocolate Meringues with Peach Sauce

Per serving:
110 cal. (4% from fat), 2 g pro., 27 g carbo., 1 g fat,
0 mg cholesterol, 2 g dietary fiber, 40 mg sodium.

Preparation time:
1 hour

Baking time:
35 minutes

Cooling time:
1 hour

The crisp chocolate meringues can be made ahead and stored in a sealed Tupperware® container up to three days at room temperature. The meringues also will keep for two weeks in the freezer. To thaw, let them stand at room temperature for 30 minutes.

2   egg whites

½   teaspoon vanilla

¼   teaspoon cream of tartar

    Dash salt

½   cup sugar

¼   cup unsweetened cocoa powder, sifted

½   cup apple juice

2   teaspoons cornstarch

⅛   teaspoon grated fresh nutmeg or ground nutmeg

1½ cups frozen unsweetened peach slices, thawed

- Let egg whites stand at room temperature in a small mixing bowl for 30 minutes. Cover a baking sheet with plain brown paper. Draw six 3-inch circles 2 inches apart on the brown paper. Set aside.

- Add vanilla, cream of tartar, and salt to whites. Beat with an electric mixer on medium speed until soft peaks form (tips curl). Add sugar, 1 tablespoon at a time, beating on high speed until stiff peaks form (tips stand straight) and sugar is almost dissolved. Fold in cocoa powder.

- Use a spoon to spread meringue mixture over circles on paper, building sides higher than centers to form shells.

- Bake in 300° oven for 35 minutes. Turn off oven and let shells cool and dry in oven with door closed for 1 hour.

- Meanwhile, combine juice, cornstarch, and nutmeg in saucepan. Stir in peaches. Cook and stir until thickened and bubbly. Cook and stir 2 minutes more. Cover; chill.

- To serve, place meringue shells on dessert plates. Spoon peach mixture into shells. Makes 6 servings.

Meringues Made Easy

Not only are meringues delicious, they also contain no fat or cholesterol. For a meringue that fluffs rather than flops, follow these simple steps:

Start with a clean glass or metal mixing bowl and beaters. After separating the egg whites, let them stand at room temperature about 30 minutes. Then beat the egg whites with an electric mixer on medium speed until soft peaks form (tips curl) before adding sugar. Beating the egg whites too much or too little before adding the sugar may give you unsatisfactory volume.

After gradually adding the sugar, continue beating the egg whites just until glossy stiff peaks form (tips stand straight). If you beat the whites too much at this stage, the baked meringue will be dull; beat the whites too little, and the meringue will shrink excessively after baking.

Shape or pipe the beaten egg whites immediately to maintain maximum volume.

Cinnamon Fruit Compote

Per serving:
69 cal. (4% from fat), 1 g pro., 17 g carbo., 0 g fat,
0 mg cholesterol, 2 g dietary fiber, 4 mg sodium.

**Preparation time:
30 minutes**

**Chilling time:
2 hours**

Layer fresh fruits in a pretty glass bowl for a simply elegant dessert. Just before serving, pour the lightly spiced syrup over the fruit and sprinkle with shredded orange peel.

¾ cup white grape juice

1 tablespoon sugar

2 inches stick cinnamon

2 whole nutmegs

1 teaspoon finely shredded orange peel

1 cup strawberries, halved

2 medium nectarines, pitted and sliced

1 cup seedless green grapes

1 11-ounce can mandarin orange sections, drained

Shredded orange peel (optional)

- Combine grape juice, sugar, stick cinnamon, whole nutmegs, and the 1 teaspoon orange peel in a small saucepan. Cook over medium heat, stirring constantly, until sugar dissolves. Bring to boiling; reduce heat. Cover and simmer for 5 minutes. Remove from heat. Cool for 15 minutes. Remove cinnamon and nutmegs. Chill at least 2 hours.

- To serve, layer *half* of the strawberries and all of the nectarines, grapes, and orange sections in a large glass bowl. Top with remaining strawberries.

- Pour white grape juice mixture over fruit. Garnish compote with additional shredded orange peel, if desired. Makes 8 servings.

Mint-Chocolate Chip Ice Milk

Per serving:
94 cal. (11% from fat), 4 g pro., 16 g carbo., 1 g fat,
15 mg cholesterol, 0 g dietary fiber, 53 mg sodium.

**Preparation time:
20 minutes**

**Chilling time:
1 hour**

**Freezing time:
25 minutes (in ice cream freezer)**

This lighter version of ice cream uses just one whole egg and skim milk in place of whole milk or cream.

¾ cup sugar

1 envelope unflavored gelatin

1 12-ounce can evaporated skim milk

1 egg white

1 egg

2½ cups skim milk

2 tablespoons white crème de menthe or ¼ teaspoon mint flavoring

2 teaspoons vanilla

Several drops green food coloring (optional)

1½ ounces semisweet chocolate, chopped

- Stir together sugar and gelatin in a large saucepan. Stir in the evaporated skim milk. Cook and stir over medium-low heat until sugar and gelatin dissolve and mixture almost boils; remove from heat.

- Combine egg white and egg in a small mixing bowl and beat slightly. Stir *about ½ cup* of the hot gelatin mixture into slightly beaten egg mixture; return all to saucepan. Cook, stirring constantly, over low heat 2 minutes more. *Do not boil.* Stir the 2½ cups skim milk, the crème de menthe or mint flavoring, and vanilla into cooked mixture. Cover and chill in refrigerator for 1 hour.

- Stir food coloring into cooled milk mixture, if desired. Stir in chopped chocolate.

- Freeze in a 4- to 5-quart ice cream freezer according to manufacturer's directions. Makes 16 (½-cup) servings.

Cinnamon Fruit Compote

Poached Pears in Wine Sauce

Per serving:
165 cal. (3% from fat), 1 g pro., 33 g carbo., 1 g fat,
0 mg cholesterol, 5 g dietary fiber, 3 mg sodium.

Preparation time:
25 minutes

Chilling time:
2 hours

Some of the best things in life are virtually fat-free! For best results, use firm pears for poaching.

1 cup rosé wine or orange juice

2 tablespoons sugar

3 inches stick cinnamon

2 teaspoons lemon juice

6 whole cloves

4 medium pears

Fresh mint sprigs (optional)

- Stir together wine or orange juice, sugar, cinnamon, lemon juice, and cloves in a large skillet.

- Meanwhile, halve pears lengthwise, leaving stem attached to one half. Carefully remove core from halves, leaving stems attached. With skin side up, use a sharp knife to cut pear halves into thin slices, cutting almost, but not quite, to the stem end.

- Bring wine mixture to boiling. Place pear halves, skin side up, in skillet. Return mixture to boiling; reduce heat. Cover and simmer about 7 minutes or until pears are just tender. Use a slotted spoon to remove pears from skillet. Place pear halves in dessert dishes.

- Boil wine mixture, uncovered, in skillet for 3 to 4 minutes or until reduced to ¼ cup. Remove cinnamon and cloves. Pour wine mixture over pears. Cover and chill at least 2 hours. Garnish with mint sprigs, if desired. Makes 4 servings.

Spicy Fruit Cup

Per serving:
90 cal. (3% from fat), 1 g pro., 23 g carbo., 0 g fat,
0 mg cholesterol, 2 g dietary fiber, 4 mg sodium.

Preparation time:
15 minutes

Chilling time:
2 hours

No sugar, just spice in this especially nice fruit compote.

1 8-ounce can pineapple chunks (juice pack)

½ cup orange juice

⅛ teaspoon ground cinnamon

Dash ground nutmeg

2 tablespoons dry white wine (optional)

1 medium pear

1 cup fresh strawberries, halved

1 11-ounce can mandarin orange sections, drained

1 8-ounce can grapefruit sections (juice pack), drained

- Stir together *undrained* pineapple, orange juice, cinnamon, and nutmeg in a medium mixing bowl. Stir in white wine, if desired.

- Core and slice pear. Add pear slices, strawberries, mandarin orange sections, and grapefruit sections to the pineapple mixture. Cover and chill mixture for 2 to 6 hours. Divide the fruit mixture among 6 dessert dishes. Makes 6 servings.

Cake Brownies

Per serving:
66 cal. (28% from fat), 1 g pro., 12 g carbo., 2 g fat,
0 mg cholesterol, 0 g dietary fiber, 33 mg sodium.

Preparation time:
10 minutes

Baking time:
16 minutes

Cooling time:
1½ hours

Standing time:
30 minutes

Finally! Brownies even dieters can afford to splurge on. Drizzled with chocolate icing, these brownies taste anything except low-fat!

Nonstick spray coating

¼ cup margarine

⅔ cup granulated sugar

¼ cup unsweetened cocoa powder

1 egg white

½ teaspoon vanilla

¾ cup all-purpose flour

⅓ cup skim milk

¼ teaspoon baking powder

¼ teaspoon baking soda

1 teaspoon powdered sugar

Chocolate Icing (see recipe at right)

- Spray a 9x9x2-inch baking pan with nonstick coating.

- Melt margarine in saucepan. Remove from heat. Stir in granulated sugar and cocoa powder until combined.

- Add egg white and vanilla to saucepan. Using a wooden spoon, lightly beat just until combined. Add flour, milk, baking powder, and baking soda. Beat with the spoon until well combined. Spread batter into prepared pan.

- Bake in a 350° oven for 16 to 18 minutes or until a wooden toothpick inserted near the center comes out clean. Cool in pan on a wire rack. Sprinkle with powdered sugar. Drizzle with Chocolate Icing and let stand about 30 minutes or until icing is set. Cut into bars. Makes 24 servings.

Chocolate Icing: Combine ½ cup sifted *powdered sugar*, 1 tablespoon unsweetened *cocoa powder*, and ¼ teaspoon *vanilla* in a small mixing bowl. Stir in enough *skim milk* (1 to 2 tablespoons) to make icing of drizzling consistency.

The Scoop on Frozen Desserts

The freezer section of your supermarket is full of ice cream-like treats. Which is best for a healthful diet? Check these choices:

Ice cream: This silky smooth dessert is made with at least 10 percent milk fat, so you'd be wise to avoid it if you are watching your weight. Some of the premium brands are especially dangerous for dieters: Their fat content goes well beyond the 10 percent mark.

Low-fat or light ice cream: This kissing cousin to ice cream has the same flavor and texture but a lower fat content (3 to 5 percent milk fat).

Frozen yogurt: The fat content of this product varies, because no federal standards have been set for it. Read the label; some brands are similar to regular ice cream while others are more like low-fat or light ice cream.

Sherbet: This fruity dessert contains 1 to 2 percent milk fat. To offset the tangy flavor from the fruits used, more sweetening often is added to sherbets than to other frozen desserts.

Lower-calorie ice cream-like products: Fat substitutes replace all or part of the milk fat in these frozen desserts. Brands vary widely in fat content; be sure to read the label.

Lighter Apple Strudel

Lighter Apple Strudel

Per serving:
131 cal. (18% from fat), 3 g pro., 25 g carbo., 3 g fat,
0 mg cholesterol, 1 g dietary fiber, 99 mg sodium.

Preparation time:
40 minutes

Baking time:
30 minutes

Cooling time:
1 hour

Thanks to frozen phyllo dough, this dessert also is easier to prepare than classic strudel.

4   medium cooking apples, peeled, cored, and thinly sliced (4 cups)

1   tablespoon lemon juice

2   tablespoons granulated sugar

2   tablespoons brown sugar

1   teaspoon ground cinnamon

2   egg whites

2   tablespoons cooking oil

1   tablespoon water

12 sheets frozen phyllo dough (17x12-inch rectangles), thawed

Nonstick spray coating

2   tablespoons powdered sugar

- Sprinkle apples with lemon juice. Stir together sugars and cinnamon in a small mixing bowl.

- Combine egg whites, oil, and water in another small mixing bowl; beat with a fork until well mixed. Very lightly brush *one sheet* of phyllo with some of the egg white mixture. (Remove one sheet of phyllo at a time and keep remaining sheets covered with a damp paper towel.) Repeat brushing with 5 more sheets, stacking to make 6 layers.

- Place *half* of the apples in a 2-inch-wide strip along one long edge of phyllo stack, leaving 2 inches at short sides. Sprinkle apples with *half* of the sugar mixture. Fold in 2 inches along the short sides; roll up tightly, beginning from the long side with apples. Spray a 15x10x1-inch baking pan with nonstick coating. Place roll, seam side down, in pan.

- Repeat with remaining phyllo, egg white mixture, apples, and sugar mixture to make a second roll.

- Bake in a 350° oven for 30 to 35 minutes or until golden brown. Cool slightly; loosen from pan. Cool in pan on wire rack. Sift powdered sugar over strudel just before serving. Makes 12 servings.

Mocha Soufflé

Per serving:
118 cal. (3% from fat), 7 g pro., 22 g carbo., 0 g fat,
2 mg cholesterol, 1 g dietary fiber, 100 mg sodium.

Preparation time:
50 minutes

Baking time:
20 minutes

You don't have to be a dieter to appreciate this fabulous, fat-reduced dessert. If you can afford a few extra grams of fat, go ahead and pass a bowl of whipped dessert topping.

6   egg whites

⅓   cup sugar

3   tablespoons unsweetened cocoa powder

2   tablespoons cornstarch

1   teaspoon instant coffee crystals

1   cup evaporated skim milk

2   teaspoons vanilla

Nonstick spray coating

1   tablespoon sugar

½   teaspoon cream of tartar

- Let egg whites stand at room temperature in a large mixing bowl for 30 minutes. Meanwhile, combine the ⅓ cup sugar, the cocoa powder, cornstarch, and coffee crystals in a small saucepan. Stir in evaporated skim milk. Cook and stir over medium heat until thickened and bubbly. Remove from heat. Stir in vanilla. Cover surface of mixture with waxed paper. Set aside.

- Spray a 2-quart soufflé dish with nonstick coating. Coat sides and bottom of dish with the 1 tablespoon sugar. Set aside. Beat egg whites and cream of tartar until stiff peaks form (tips stand straight).

- Fold some of the beaten egg whites into the cocoa mixture to lighten. Gently fold into remaining beaten egg whites. Pour into prepared soufflé dish.

- Bake in a 375° oven for 20 to 25 minutes or until a knife inserted near the center comes out clean. Serve immediately. Makes 6 servings.

English Summer Fruit Pudding

Per serving:
179 cal. (3% from fat), 3 g pro., 41 g carbo., 1 g fat,
0 mg cholesterol, 3 g dietary fiber, 340 mg sodium.

Preparation time:
25 minutes

Chilling time:
8 hours

Summer-fresh raspberries
and peaches are encased in
angel cake for a deliciously
different make-ahead
dessert.

1   purchased angel cake
(about 1 pound), cut
into ½-inch-thick
slices and crusts
removed

⅓   cup orange juice or
white grape juice

¼   cup sugar

4   cups raspberries

2   cups peeled and
chopped peaches

    Raspberries (optional)

    Vanilla low-fat yogurt
(optional)

- Arrange about *three-fourths* of the cake slices on bottom and sides of a 2-quart soufflé dish, overlapping or cutting pieces to fit; set aside.

- Stir together orange juice and sugar in a small saucepan. Heat and stir just until sugar dissolves. Remove from heat. Stir in the 4 cups raspberries and the peaches. Pour fruit mixture into cake-lined soufflé dish. Cover with remaining cake slices. Cover top of dish with waxed paper. Place a heavy plate on top of waxed paper. Weigh plate down with a heavy object such as a can of fruit or a saucepan. Chill at least 8 hours.

- To serve, remove the weight, plate, and paper. Gently loosen edges with a thin-bladed knife. Invert onto serving plate. Garnish with additional raspberries and serve with yogurt, if desired. Makes 10 servings.

Lemon Cake Pudding

Per serving:
128 cal. (24% from fat), 4 g pro., 21 g carbo., 3 g fat,
73 mg cholesterol, 0 g dietary fiber, 70 mg sodium.

Preparation time:
15 minutes

Baking time:
40 minutes

Cooling time:
30 minutes

During baking, the batter
separates into an airy
sponge cake and a tangy
sauce. For the best flavor,
serve warm.

⅔   cup sugar

¼   cup all-purpose flour

    Dash salt

1   teaspoon finely
shredded lemon peel

2   tablespoons lemon
juice

1   tablespoon liquid
margarine

3   egg yolks

1   8-ounce carton plain
low-fat yogurt

½   cup skim milk

3   egg whites

- Combine sugar, flour, and salt in a medium mixing bowl. Stir in lemon peel, lemon juice, and margarine.

- Beat egg yolks thoroughly in another medium mixing bowl with a rotary beater. Beat in yogurt and milk. Stir into lemon mixture.

- Beat egg whites until stiff peaks form (tips stand straight). Fold into lemon mixture. Pour batter into an ungreased 8x8x2-inch baking pan.

- Place pan with batter in a 13x9x2-inch baking pan; place on oven rack and pour hot water into 13x9x2-inch pan to a depth of 1 inch. Bake in a 350° oven about 40 minutes or until set when lightly touched with finger. Cool on wire rack for 30 minutes. Serve warm. Serves 9.

Peppermint Angel Cake

Per serving:
181 cal. (3% from fat), 4 g pro., 42 g carbo., 1 g fat,
0 mg cholesterol, 1 g dietary fiber, 298 mg sodium.

Preparation time:
10 minutes

Baking time:
30 minutes

Cooling time:
1½ hours

Only the flavor is sinful
with this heavenly dessert,
which is made with angel
cake mix and a glorious,
guilt-free chocolate sauce.

1   16-ounce package
    angel cake mix

10 striped, round
    peppermint candies,
    finely crushed (⅓ cup)

    Fat-Free Chocolate
    Sauce (see recipe,
    below right)

    Striped, round
    peppermint candies,
    crushed (optional)

- Prepare cake mix batter according to package directions.
  Gently fold in the ⅓ cup crushed candies. Pour batter
  evenly into an ungreased 10-inch tube pan. Gently cut
  through cake batter with a knife or narrow metal spatula
  to remove any air pockets.

- Bake cake according to package directions. Immediately
  invert baked cake in the pan and cool completely. Using
  a narrow spatula, loosen sides of cake from pan. Remove
  cake from pan.

- To serve, slice cake and spoon warm Fat-Free Chocolate
  Sauce over each serving. Sprinkle with additional
  crushed peppermint candies, if desired. Chill any
  remaining sauce; reheat before serving on leftover cake.
  Makes 12 servings.

Fat-Free Chocolate Sauce: Stir together ¾ cup *sugar*,
⅓ cup unsweetened *cocoa powder,* and 4 teaspoons
cornstarch in a small saucepan. Add ½ cup *evaporated
skim milk.* Cook over medium heat, stirring constantly,
until sauce is thickened and bubbly. Cook and stir for
2 minutes more. Remove from heat. Stir in 1 teaspoon
vanilla. Cool sauce slightly.

Apricot-Oatmeal Bars

Per serving:
76 cal. (22% from fat), 1 g pro., 14 g carbo., 2 g fat,
6 mg cholesterol, 1 g dietary fiber, 47 mg sodium.

Preparation time:
15 minutes

Baking time:
20 minutes

Cooling time:
1 hour

This lightly glazed moist
bar has about half the
cooking oil of a regular bar
recipe and no margarine in
the glaze, so you're in for a
lower-fat treat.

1   cup all-purpose flour
½   cup whole wheat flour
½   teaspoon baking soda
½   teaspoon ground
     cinnamon
1   beaten egg
¼   cup packed brown
     sugar
½   cup plain low-fat yogurt
¼   cup molasses
¼   cup cooking oil
1   cup quick-cooking
     rolled oats
¾   cup snipped dried
     apricots
½   cup raisins
     Orange Glaze (see
     recipe, above right)

- Combine all-purpose flour, whole wheat flour, baking
  soda, cinnamon, and ½ teaspoon *salt* in a large mixing
  bowl. Combine egg, brown sugar, yogurt, molasses, and
  oil in medium mixing bowl; stir in ⅓ cup *water.* Stir into
  flour mixture; mix well. Stir in rolled oats, apricots, and
  raisins. Spread in a 13x9x2-inch baking pan.

- Bake in a 350° oven for 20 to 25 minutes or until a
  wooden toothpick inserted near the center comes out
  clean. Cool on a wire rack.

- Drizzle with Orange Glaze; cut into bars. Makes 36 bars.

Orange Glaze: Stir together ¾ cup sifted *powdered
sugar* and enough *orange juice* or *milk* (1 to 2
tablespoons) to make a glaze of drizzling consistency.

Raspberry Crepes

Per serving:
209 cal. (22% from fat), 6 g pro., 36 g carbo., 5 g fat,
61 mg cholesterol, 4 g dietary fiber, 81 mg sodium.

**Preparation time:
25 minutes**

Healthful eating is pure pleasure when you can indulge in desserts like this. If you like, you can make the crepes ahead (see tip, below).

2½ cups raspberries or halved strawberries

3 tablespoons granulated sugar

¾ cup skim milk

½ cup all-purpose flour

1 egg

Dash salt

Nonstick spray coating

Margarine

¼ cup dairy sour cream

4 teaspoons brown sugar

- Combine berries and granulated sugar in a medium mixing bowl. Set berries aside.

- Meanwhile, for crepes, combine milk, flour, egg, and salt in a bowl. Beat with a rotary beater until smooth.

- Spray a 6-inch skillet with nonstick coating. Place over medium heat until a drop of water sizzles. Remove from heat. Spoon in *2 tablespoons* batter. Tilt skillet to spread batter. Return to heat. Cook crepe on one side about 1 minute or until brown. Run a spatula around edge of crepe to loosen. Invert skillet and remove crepe.

- Repeat to make 8 crepes, lightly greasing skillet with margarine, as necessary.

- To serve, spread some of the sour cream over a quarter of the unbrowned side of each crepe. Place about *⅓ cup* raspberries on sour cream on *each* crepe. Sprinkle with brown sugar. Fold each crepe in half. Fold in half again, around fruit, forming a triangle. Makes 4 servings.

Convenient Crepes

Streamline dessert preparation by making crepes several days or even months ahead of when you'll use them. Or you can purchase crepes already made.

To store homemade or purchased crepes: Place two pieces of waxed paper on top of a cooked crepe; top with another crepe. Repeat to stack all the cooked crepes. Place the stack in a Tupperware® Freezer Mates® Medium 1 or Large 1 container. Store the crepes in the refrigerator for up to two days or freeze for up to four months.

Let the frozen crepes thaw in the covered container at room temperature about one hour before using.

Raspberry Crepes

Pumpkin Custards

Per serving:
104 cal. (2% from fat), 6 g pro., 20 g carbo., 0 g fat,
2 mg cholesterol, 2 g dietary fiber, 115 mg sodium.

Preparation time:
10 minutes

Baking time:
35 minutes

Cooling time:
30 minutes

Similar in taste to pumpkin pie, these individual custards are abundantly rich even without egg yolks and regular evaporated milk.

2	egg whites
1	cup canned pumpkin
¾	cup evaporated skim milk
3	tablespoons sugar
½	teaspoon ground cinnamon
⅛	teaspoon ground ginger
⅛	teaspoon ground allspice
	Dash salt
	Whipped dessert topping (optional)

- Place egg whites in a medium mixing bowl and beat until foamy. Stir in canned pumpkin, evaporated skim milk, sugar, cinnamon, ginger, allspice, and salt.

- Place four 6-ounce custard cups or ramekins in a shallow baking pan. Pour pumpkin mixture into cups.

- Place the baking pan containing the cups on oven rack. Pour *boiling water or hottest tap water* around custard cups in baking pan to a depth of 1 inch.

- Bake in a 325° oven for 35 to 40 minutes or until a knife inserted near the centers comes out clean. Remove custard cups from water. Cool on wire rack for 30 minutes and serve warm or chill before serving. Top each serving with a small spoonful of whipped dessert topping, if desired. Makes 4 servings.

Piña Colada Pudding

Per serving:
102 cal. (26% from fat), 3 g pro., 17 g carbo., 3 g fat,
1 mg cholesterol, 0 g dietary fiber, 253 mg sodium.

Preparation time:
10 minutes

Chilling time:
1 hour

Taste the tropics with each spoonful of this pineapple pudding.

1	4-serving-size package sugar-free instant vanilla pudding mix
1½	cups skim milk
1	1.3-ounce envelope whipped dessert topping mix
1	8-ounce can crushed pineapple (juice pack)
2	tablespoons coconut, toasted

- Stir together pudding mix, milk, and dessert topping mix in a small mixing bowl. Beat with an electric mixer on low speed about 30 seconds or until moistened. Beat on high speed about 2 minutes more or until thickened. Fold in *undrained* pineapple.

- Spoon pudding mixture into 6 dessert dishes. Sprinkle each serving with toasted coconut. Chill at least 1 hour. Makes 6 servings.

Ambrosia Pudding

Per serving:
139 cal. (24% from fat), 3 g pro., 25 g carbo., 4 g fat,
1 mg cholesterol, 1 g dietary fiber, 60 mg sodium.

Preparation time:
15 minutes

Cooling time:
15 minutes

Chilling time:
4 hours

Spoon luscious low-calorie vanilla pudding over mandarin oranges and sprinkle with toasted coconut for a refreshing, ambrosia-flavored dessert.

2	tablespoons sugar
1	tablespoon cornstarch
1	cup skim milk
1	tablespoon margarine
1	teaspoon vanilla
1	medium banana
1	11-ounce can mandarin orange sections, drained
2	tablespoons coconut, toasted

● Stir together sugar and cornstarch in a small saucepan. Stir in skim milk. Cook and stir until mixture is thickened and bubbly. Cook and stir for 2 minutes more. Remove from heat. Stir in margarine and vanilla. Cool 15 minutes. Cover and chill for 4 to 6 hours.

● Slice banana. Divide banana slices and mandarin oranges among 4 dessert dishes. Spoon some of pudding mixture over fruit in each dish. Sprinkle each serving with toasted coconut. Makes 4 servings.

Fresh Fruit Know-How

There's no better choice for a healthful dessert than fresh fruit. Fruits should be plump, tender, brightly colored, and heavy for their size (this indicates juiciness). Avoid fruits with mold, mildew, bruises, cuts, or other blemishes.

To ripen apricots, plums, peaches, nectarines, pears, or melons, place in a paper bag and let stand at room temperature for a few days or until ripe. Then store the ripened fruit in the refrigerator.

Certain fruits are better certain times of the year. Here's when to look for what:

Fresh Fruits	Peak Availability
Apples	Year-round
Apricots	May–August
Berries	June–August
Melons	Year-round
Peaches	June–September
Pears	Year-round
Plums	June–September
Rhubarb	February–May

Orange-Banana-Pineapple Sorbet,
Cranberry-Raspberry Sorbet, and
Lemon-Mint Sorbet

Orange-Banana-Pineapple Sorbet

Per serving:
72 cal. (1% from fat), 1 g pro., 18 g carbo., 0 g fat,
0 mg cholesterol, 0 g dietary fiber, 1 mg sodium.

Preparation time:
20 minutes

Freezing time:
30 minutes (in ice cream freezer)

Prepare a trio of frozen desserts from three different frozen fruit juice concentrates. For an impressive presentation, serve mini scoops of all three ices layered in goblets, as shown opposite.

2¾ cups water

¼ cup sugar

½ of a 12-ounce can (¾ cup) frozen orange-banana-pineapple juice concentrate or orange juice concentrate

1 teaspoon finely shredded orange peel

- Combine water and sugar in a small saucepan. Heat and stir until sugar is dissolved. Cool to room temperature.

- Add frozen concentrate and orange peel. Stir until concentrate is dissolved. Freeze in a 1- or 2-quart ice cream freezer according to the manufacturer's directions. Makes about 8 (½-cup) servings.

Lemon-Mint Sorbet: Prepare fruit Sorbet as directed above, *except* add 1 cup fresh *mint leaves*, crushed, to the dissolved sugar-water mixture. Cover and simmer for 10 minutes more. Strain into a large mixing bowl; discard mint. Continue as directed, *except* substitute one 6-ounce can frozen *lemonade concentrate* for the orange-banana-pineapple juice concentrate and finely shredded *lemon peel* for the finely shredded orange peel. (The nutrition information per serving is the same as above *except:* 63 cal., 0 g pro., 16 g carbo.)

Cranberry-Raspberry Sorbet: Prepare fruit Sorbet as directed above, *except* increase the sugar to ½ *cup*, substitute half of a 12-ounce can frozen *cranberry-raspberry juice concentrate* for the frozen orange-banana-pineapple juice concentrate, and omit finely shredded orange peel. (The nutrition information per serving is the same as above *except:* 103 cal. (0% from fat), 0 g pro., 27 g carbo., 0 mg sodium.)

Black Cherry Sorbet

Per serving:
148 cal. (4% from fat), 1 g pro., 33 g carbo., 1 g fat,
0 mg cholesterol, 1 g dietary fiber, 2 mg sodium.

Preparation time:
20 minutes

Freezing times:
4 hours; 6 hours

Make any occasion special with this cherry-and-champagne-flavored ice. Dress up each serving with a single long-stemmed cherry.

5 cups pitted dark sweet cherries

1 cup water

½ cup water

1 cup sugar

1 cup champagne or sparkling white grape juice

2 teaspoons finely shredded lemon peel

- Combine cherries and the 1 cup water in a blender container or food processor bowl. Cover and blend or process until pureed. Strain cherry mixture through a sieve, discarding pulp.

- Combine strained cherry mixture, the ½ cup water, the sugar, champagne or sparkling grape juice, and lemon peel in a large mixing bowl, stirring until sugar dissolves. Pour into a 13x9x2-inch baking pan. Cover and freeze about 4 hours or until almost firm.

- Meanwhile, chill a large mixing bowl. Break the frozen mixture into chunks. Transfer chunks to the mixing bowl. Beat with an electric mixer on medium speed until mixture is smooth but not melted. Return quickly to the cold pan. Cover and freeze for 6 to 8 hours more or until sorbet is firm. Makes 10 (½-cup) servings.

Choco-Orange Mousse

Per serving:
90 cal. (30% from fat), 3 g pro., 13 g carbo., 3 g fat,
1 mg cholesterol, 0 g dietary fiber, 252 mg sodium.

Preparation time:
10 minutes

Chilling time:
2 hours

Make this sophisticated mousse from dessert topping mix, sugar-free chocolate pudding mix, and a splash of orange juice. Fold in miniature chocolate chips for a decadent dessert that lacks only the calories.

1 1.3-ounce envelope whipped dessert topping mix

1½ cups cold skim milk

½ cup orange juice

1 4-serving-size package sugar-free instant chocolate pudding mix

1 tablespoon miniature semisweet chocolate pieces

Orange peel curls (optional)

● Combine topping mix and ½ *cup* of the milk in a medium mixing bowl. Beat with an electric mixer on high speed about 2 minutes or until mixture forms stiff peaks (tips stand straight).

● Add remaining milk, orange juice, and chocolate pudding mix. Beat with an electric mixer on low speed just until mixed. Beat on medium speed about 2 minutes more or until well mixed. Fold in chocolate pieces.

● Spoon chocolate mixture into 6 dessert dishes. Chill at least 2 hours. Garnish each serving with an orange peel curl, if desired. Makes 6 servings.

Desserts You Can Sip

Instead of something to eat for dessert, try a steaming cup of coffee or tea.

Check the selection of coffees available at the supermarket and at specialty coffee shops. You'll find a wide variety of coffees, from decaffeinated to espresso. Some are flavored with spices, others with nuts or chocolate.

Dress up a cup of coffee with a dollop of thawed frozen whipped dessert topping and a sprinkling of ground cinnamon, nutmeg, mace, or cardamom. (A tablespoon of the whipped dessert topping adds about 15 calories.)

Flavored teas are another possible finalé. Look for fruit- and spice-flavored varieties at the supermarket.

Ginger-Almond Flan

Per serving:
109 cal. (23% from fat), 8 g pro., 14 g carbo., 3 g fat,
73 mg cholesterol, 0 g dietary fiber, 118 mg sodium.

Preparation time:
10 minutes

Baking time:
30 minutes

Cooling time:
1½ hours

Indulge in these silky, smooth custards without worrying about calories or fat. We capitalize on egg whites, skim milk, and just a hint of honey for sweetness.

4 egg whites

2 eggs

2 cups skim milk

3 tablespoons honey

1½ teaspoons vanilla

½ teaspoon ground ginger

Few drops almond extract

Dash salt

2 tablespoons sliced almonds, toasted

● Combine egg whites, eggs, milk, honey, vanilla, ginger, almond extract, and salt. Beat with a rotary beater until well combined but not foamy. Place six 6-ounce custard cups in a 13x9x2-inch baking pan on an oven rack. Pour egg mixture into custard cups. Pour *boiling water or hottest tap water* into the baking pan around cups to a depth of 1 inch.

● Bake in a 325° oven 30 to 40 minutes or until a knife inserted near centers comes out clean. Cool on a wire rack. Chill thoroughly, if desired. Serve topped with toasted almonds. Makes 6 servings.

Lemon Puffs

Per serving:
97 cal. (26% from fat), 5 g pro., 13 g carbo., 3 g fat,
107 mg cholesterol, 0 g dietary fiber, 54 mg sodium.

Preparation time:
20 minutes

Baking time:
8 minutes

Sprinkle this soufflé-like dessert with powdered sugar and whisk it straight to the table. For an elegant orange puff, substitute orange juice and peel for the lemon.

Nonstick spray coating

2 egg yolks

2 teaspoons all-purpose flour

4 egg whites

½ teaspoon finely shredded lemon peel

2 tablespoons lemon juice

1 teaspoon vanilla

3 tablespoons granulated sugar

1 tablespoon powdered sugar

● Generously spray a 2-quart square baking dish with nonstick coating. Set aside. Beat egg yolks with an electric mixer on high speed about 2 minutes or until well combined. Fold in flour. Set aside.

● Wash and dry beaters thoroughly. Place egg whites, lemon peel, lemon juice, and vanilla in a large mixing bowl. Beat with an electric mixer on medium speed until soft peaks form. Gradually add granulated sugar, beating on high speed until stiff peaks form (tips stand straight).

● Fold some of the egg white mixture into yolk mixture. Gently fold yolk mixture into remaining beaten egg whites. Spoon mixture into prepared baking dish, forming 4 even mounds.

● Bake in a 375° oven for 8 to 10 minutes or until puffs are golden and a knife inserted near the centers comes out clean. Sift powdered sugar over the puffs. Serve immediately. Makes 4 servings.

Index

Index (continued)

NUTRITIONAL FACTS

So you can keep track of what you eat, each recipe in this book lists the nutritional values for one serving. Here's how we made our analyses.

When a recipe gives a choice of ingredients (such as margarine or butter), we used the first choice in our analysis.

Ingredients listed as optional were omitted from our calculations.

Finally, we rounded all values to the nearest whole number.